WITHDRAWN

Children of War

CHILDREN OF WAR

Roger Rosenblatt

ANCHOR PRESS / DOUBLEDAY
GARDEN CITY, NEW YORK
1983

This Anchor Press edition is the first publication of *Children of War*, which was based on a *Time* magazine article of January 11, 1982. All photographs in this book have been reproduced by permission of Time Inc.

Chapter One, "Preparations for a Journey," first appeared in *The Hudson Review*, Vol. XXXVI, No. 1 (Spring 1983).

Chapter Six, "Cambodia," first appeared in slightly different form with the title "The Road to Kaho I Dang" in *The Yale Review*, Vol. 3 (April, 1983).

Grateful acknowledgment is made for permission to include the lyrics from the following copyrighted song.

"Any Dream Will Do." Words by Tim Rice from *Joseph and the Amazing Technicolor Dreamcoat* by Andrew Lloyd Webber and Tim Rice. Published and reproduced by permission of Novello & Company, Ltd. copyright © 1969 by Novello & Company, Ltd.

Library of Congress Cataloging in Publication Data
Rosenblatt, Roger.
Children of war.
1. Children and war. 2. Pacifism. I. Title.
HQ784.W3R67   1983   305.2′3
ISBN 0-385-18250-3

Library of Congress Catalog Card Number 82-45366
Copyright © 1983 by Roger Rosenblatt

FOR GINNY, CARL, AMY AND JOHN

ACKNOWLEDGMENTS

Many of those to whom I owe thanks will find their names in the text where I hope their generous contributions are evident. Others who lent this book their knowledge and wisdom are Henry Grunwald and Ralph Graves, who commented on and improved the manuscript; Richard Duncan and William Mader, who worked out the itinerary for my journey; Brigid O'Hara-Forster, who shaped and guided much of the original magazine story; Frank Trippett, Stephen Smith, Walter Kaiser and Nora Ephron, who provided indispensable words of advice; Jeanne-Marie North, who did everything from scholarly research to emergency typing, all expertly; and other friends and colleagues at *Time*—Michele Stephenson, Rudy Hoglund, Arnold Drapkin, David Halevy, Nafez Nazzal, Aporanee Buatang, Marlin Levin and Mirka Gondicas—who helped in various essential ways. It is an honor to know and work with such people.

CONTENTS

ONE	PREPARATIONS FOR A JOURNEY	13
TWO	BELFAST	27
THREE	ISRAEL	55
FOUR	PALESTINIANS	85
FIVE	PAUSING WITH TELEMACHOS	111
SIX	CAMBODIA	125
SEVEN	VIET NAM	151
EPILOGUE	INTO THE FIRE	181

CHILDREN OF WAR

O N E

Preparations
for a Journey

The last child I spoke with was Trinh, though she did not see
me at first, and I, at first, did not address her. I was preoccu-
pied with the priest, and she with Hong Kong Island. Standing
quietly by herself on a corner of the pontoon, she stared open-
mouthed across the blue harbor at the silver office buildings
pressed tight against Victoria Peak in whose windows the sun
seemed to burn. There were no such astonishing towers in
Haiphong, the home Trinh left thirty-five days earlier with her
mother, her brothers and sisters, and the priest. In all there
had been fifty-one aboard, most of them belonging to the Catholic community of Haiphong. Although they had been stowed in
holds intended for fish and the junk had nearly sunk three
times, theirs had not been a harrowing voyage, as these voyages go. Trinh showed none of the scars of other boat children,
no boils or bald patches. Indeed, she looked so alert and rested,
you would have thought she had come to greet the junk, instead of having sailed on it.

They had started out from Haiphong on September 13, one

13

day before I began my own journey. In the time between then and October 18, the date of their arrival in Hong Kong, they had traversed the South China Sea, and I half the world, having stopped and traveled in Northern Ireland, Israel, Lebanon, Thailand, and now Hong Kong. My purpose was to write a story for *Time* magazine about children growing up in the world's war zones. I went to Thailand to meet Cambodian children, who were located in refugee camps there, and to Hong Kong to talk with the Vietnamese. This hot, bright Sunday would be my last day in that city. On the pontoon the new arrivals squatted and huddled together under a tent made of shirts in order to keep the sun off. They sipped water from an orange plastic bucket which they passed from hand to hand, and gazed straight ahead, as if posing for a family photograph. Behind them their junk bobbed crazily in the harbor, giving an idea of how it must have rolled in open swells. By evening they would be processed by the Hong Kong immigration authorities, and I would be on my way home to New York.

For the moment there was eight-year-old Trinh, ogling her new world, paying no attention whatever to the gawkers in pleasure boats who circled the pontoon, peering at the strange people. Perhaps we looked like news. Beside the American with the yellow writing pad there was a photographer festooned with cameras and long lenses, and a Vietnamese interpreter. The photographer, Matthew Naythons, had been my guide and companion both in Thailand and Hong Kong. The interpreter, Le Ba Nhon, a former Vietnamese Nationalist civil servant who was imprisoned by the Viet Cong, had himself escaped from Viet Nam some months before. The three of us formed a shifting triangle around the priest and the children, Matthew taking pictures, I asking the questions I had been asking for the past five weeks, about death, hate, revenge and forgiveness.

Then with Nhon's help I called to Trinh. In an effort to put her at ease, I told her how lovely she looked in her yellow barrette. At that she turned to me, her face suddenly drained of the enthralled expression it bore a few moments earlier. Slowly her eyes filled with large, bulb-shaped tears. "She is self-conscious," Nhon explained. My blunder. Rapidly I tried to recoup.

"Trinh," I asked. "Why are you crying?"

The girl looked away. "I am crying for my father who is home in Viet Nam."

When Trinh started to cry, so did Nhon. Nhon had left his young wife and three-year-old son behind when he fled Saigon. When Nhon started to cry, so did Matthew. When Matthew started to cry, so did I. To that point I had not cried once on the trip, nor had I ever felt the urge to do so, in spite of seeing and hearing things that might justify tears. Compared with the sorrow of most of the other children I met, Trinh's was minor. Nonetheless, there were the four of us, crying noiselessly and steadily on a blue playful morning in Hong Kong Harbor for perhaps half a minute. I cannot say why.

Around us the boats of the harbor chugged and cruised—police boats, water taxis, sampans poled by old women in straw hats, ferries, tugs, dredges, schooners, container ships. Freighters with exotic names lay at anchor stolidly, like presiding judges. The only sound on the pontoon was that of the water lapping against it. I looked to the west. In a few hours the sun that would dip bloodshot below the horizon would come up white over my own children. I concluded that the world is round. I thought then that if anyone were to ask me what I learned on my trip, I would tell him that the world is round.

The idea for taking this journey first occurred to me one night in the spring of 1981 when I was struck with a peculiar and obvious fact. There are places in the world like Northern Ireland, Israel, Lebanon, Cambodia and Viet Nam that have been at war for the past twenty years or more. Therefore, the children living in these places have known nothing but war in their experience. The elements of war—explosions, destructions, dismemberments, eruptions, noises, fires, death, separation, torture, grief—which ought to be extraordinary and temporary for any life, are for these children normal and constant. Everything

15

they understand, they have learned in an atmosphere of wildness and danger. Everything they feel and sense occurs in a situation where their lives may be ruined any moment.

Who are these children? What and how do they think about the world? What opinions do they hold of their parents, of adults in general, of each other? What does friendship mean to them? Honor, loyalty? How sophisticated is their understanding of politics? Do they believe in rules, in governments, in God? Who is their God? And so forth, the questions peeling off one after another as I began to see that if the answer to the first question was that these are very special children indeed, then in the process of seeking them out, one would almost be searching a separate civilization, one that showed the external marks of children everywhere, but one that also, because of its fierce circumstances, bore a resemblance to no other. It turned out that this was so. By the end of the journey I was certain that if it were possible to airlift Trinh and all the children I had met from their various war zones and plunk them down in a neutral place, they would recognize each other immediately.

I proposed the idea of writing about these children to my editors at *Time,* who then made the story practicable by assigning three photographers to different parts of the journey, and by enlisting the help of the *Time* news bureaus in the countries on my itinerary. The basic questions of the story did not seem terribly difficult to pursue. Only as I went about preparing for the journey did I realize that this venture involved other questions as well, questions more grandiose and speculative, but which had to be asked, at least of oneself.

The children I planned to seek out live in nations and regions that are important to the world's equilibrium and safety. If one reached an understanding of who these children are, could one also get a sense of the future of their countries and peoples? Also, the wars in these areas are of several types: religious, economic, civil, ideological, sectarian feuds, wars of defense, of territorial gain, wars of deep historical hatred, and combinations of these. Would the children offer a way of grasping the meaning of war not provided by military histories and theoreticians? Finally, all modern generations are made up of children of one war or another. Could I, by talking with these people, learn where and why violence grows in the heart? This question was the least likely to get answered, but it was the loudest of the lot.

All such ponderings sounded neat and clear in the beginning, but in fact the prospect of discovering anything at all on this trip was questionable. If one really wanted to determine the future of a nation or of a region, or to learn something of the nature of warfare or of violence, there is plenty to gain from grown-ups. Why ask children? Of all the inhabitants of an area, children are, as a class, the least informed, the least concerned about world movements or world leaders, the least attentive to the nuances of public statements and discernible trends and the other means by which one's times are assessed. The dullest grown-up will usually have at least something useful to say about his world, whereas a child will often shrug away a general question, or tell you straight out that he doesn't know the answer and has never thought about the question. Admirable as such candor is, it does not teach much, unless one is so persuaded of the innate wisdom of children that every grunt becomes a cipher.

No, the reason I thought that children might suggest answers to these questions was simply that children are vitally important to adults. One way or another, most grown-ups wish to say something to the world by speaking to or through their children; and the children, as objects of this desire, are in a strong position to know what the world is like. Their great advantage is passivity. Posing no physical or social threat, they take and adjust to whatever is provided them. Their elders, in turn, give them everything they have to offer: love, custom, cruelty, ethics, knowledge, taste, fear, and, for my purposes, peace and war.

"Never take a mean advantage of anyone in a transaction," Dickens wrote his son Plom. "Be not made an ass to carry the burden of other men," Walter Raleigh told his boy. Nicola Sacco to his thirteen-year-old Dante: "Help the weak ones that cry for help." In all such instruction there seems something both brave and pathetic, self-confident and shaky that could be addressed to no one but a child. In one sense the counsel proffered is an act of heroism, the rescue of an innocent from the sins of the world or of the father. In another sense it seems a seeking of forgiveness from the child himself, as if the mere gesture of confronting a supposedly unblemished mind will end in self-purification. So divorced is the child's own life from most of the advice heaped on him that the words seem soliloquies, but in fact the child's existence as listener is essential to the grown-up's purpose. This is probably why children are used as mediums in seances—because they are thought good conductors, to have God's ear, to be passive receptacles for the world's truth.

Why are we so eager to know what someone was like or looked like as a baby, except to suggest that the baby holds the key to the grown-up's character? Freud did this to us, but so did Dr. Spock. The statement that everybody was once a child bestows instantaneous exculpation. Children are not only important to adults objectively; we are important to ourselves as children. Watch anyone tell of some discovery he made as a child. He becomes rejuvenated on the spot. His eyes brighten to the borders, the lines vanish from his forehead. It is a constant wonder to him, that childhood of his, no matter how happy, lonely or ordinary. In our heads, still playing or weeping, is the child we were. He will be preserved in place until the last moments we know, perhaps because childhood is when we liked ourselves the most, when there was the least reason or capacity for self-recrimination.

Children are given prominent positions in parades to make a show of continuity. Politicians kiss them to suggest their own virtue. Children's faces fill charity posters, because the heart melts quickest at the sight of a needy child. And the heart is acritical. Gainsborough, Renoir, Velázquez, all counted on a reflex adoration of the children they painted. Families of entertainers (singers, jugglers, comedians) feature children because they testify to the wholesomeness of the elders. The Quakers called themselves the Children of Light, as other religious and political groups call themselves the children of this or that, to claim possession of a favored and blessed state. Jesus, in a sense, was symbolized by childhood before he demonstrated his goodness as a man, because that goodness was presumed in the appearance of the infant. That, of course, is the central symbol: goodness, innocence and implicitly, redemption.

So would it be, I assumed, in the inflamed places on my journey, where war is the major industry, where all the parades, charities, politicians, parents, artists, entertainers, and even the redeemers are involved in war. Would not the children in the war zones be used as symbols too, lined up neatly at the heads of funeral processions, pressed close to the speakers at political rallies, hoisted high in the air by demagogues, photographed slain or wounded to emphasize the barbarism of the enemy? Did the children recognize their usefulness to various causes? Did they mind? Did they acknowledge that every symbol is a weapon, and thus in places where weapons are indispensable, that they were also indispensable, as instruments of guilt?

A twelve-year-old boy I visited in Belfast sat on a couch with his mother and pointed to the red crease where the British soldier's plastic bullet entered his jaw. When I asked him what he intended to do when he grew up, he answered, after some thought, that he might wish to join the IRA. His mother, a gigantic woman with blond close-cropped hair, who had been nodding demurely at everything to that point, flushed deep with desperation and sputtered: "Oh, Paul doesn't mean it." Paul meant it. He had two different injuries to display that afternoon, one to his face and the other spiritual. His mother read both properly as accusations.

This is not to say that the importance of children rests solely in what is done to them. Children see things interestingly on their own. But they do not see things the way we would see

19

them were we in their place, had we the time and leisure, say, to press our faces against our windows and stare day after day at a single scene, as children do. On this journey I saw many children at many windows—apartment house windows, terrace house windows, bus windows, truck windows, the windows of dirt huts and tents, windows with curtains and bars, windows with and without glass. Had I asked any of the children what they saw through their windows, they might have described the scene, but we both would have known that that was not the true answer. What children most often do at windows is simply to stake out a vantage point for looking at the world, which then becomes their place in the world, a secure and basically unchanging place which they use for looking at themselves.

In such positions they exercise the powers of observation that make them valuable witnesses, but these powers are rarely concentrated on hard information. Ask a child at the window what is out there, and he might possibly present a picture in detail, but then, just as likely, he might not. For a thousand hours or more, on and off, he has looked at nothing but that hill, or tree, or streetlamp. Somewhere in his memory he knows every line and dot of the objects. Yet in response to your question, he says flatly, "A hill." It is not that he has no mind for accuracy, only that he prefers to think in generalities. Before the journey I only suspected this was so. After it I was convinced. Children like to deal in abstractions; they feel comfortable with them. They may draw them from the lines and dots they take in, but the process is mysterious and labyrinthine. The product, however, is usually stunningly clear, which is why children (when they do so at all) make better witnesses to the truth than to the facts.

Children also take things seriously. Grown-ups take things seriously too, including children, but not exactly in the way that children do. When an adult takes something seriously he expresses himself demonstratively, because he wishes the world to know it, or perhaps because he wants to prove his seriousness to himself. He writes, talks, paints or gives a speech. A child, in contrast, takes things seriously by concentrating solely on the act, whatever the act may be. Nietzsche once defined a test of a man's maturity as resting in his acquiring again the seriousness of a child at play. That is it precisely. A child in a game is a spine surgeon, a Wallenda. Nothing infiltrates his imagination.

I remember a cool white morning in the north of Israel at the Manara kibbutz. This radiant kibbutz was a shelling target for the PLO in southern Lebanon, and it had been hit several times. Eddie Adams, the photographer who was with me in the Middle East, wanted to get a picture of a child playing in the cab of an old truck that had been painted pink and yellow and converted to a playground toy. The boy selected for this event was a three-year-old towhead whose face had an immense and blatant capacity for mischief. He took to his assignment with one leap and situated himself in what was clearly a familiar position for him, behind the truck's wheel. At first the boy could not take his eyes off Eddie and his cameras, an old hazard for photographers. Eddie, a gruff and sentimental man who likes to look haggard, kept telling the boy, "Play! Play!" But the boy could not play, not on command, and especially not on exhibit. He exaggerated each gesture, and smiled too wide, quite deliberately. He knew the difference between real and false games, as did Eddie, which is why Eddie also knew that the picture would never work out. Had the boy been on his own and Eddie been able to spy, it would have been another story. As it was, it seemed as if the grown-ups present were being told, politely through indirection, that one does not adulterate pure play for the sake of a photograph.

In a source of information this sense of seriousness is invaluable. It suggests that nothing is undertaken except for its own interest and worth. Children make terrible liars on the whole, not because they have a more heightened sense of morality than adults but because they pay such absolute, amazed attention to the truth that a lie becomes an insult to their sense of appreciation. It is as if they lie poorly as an apology to the truth. When they are not lying, and are thus comfortable, they usually let themselves go totally: You see, this happened, then that happened, and it was all astonishing.

Death is one of the things that children take most seriously. Not that adults take death lightly, but they do try to tame it. This is done, it is said, in order to prove that death is a continuous part of life, to make death easier to deal with by facing it squarely. Children are all for facing death squarely, but they do not regard it as a continuous part of life. To a child death is the archenemy of life, an absolute calamity. It is the beginning of nothing but emptiness and absence, prolonged and lengthening absence, and with the increasing distance all the pain of acknowledging that fact doubling and redoubling.

The Palestinian girl who, at the age of five, woke up on the floor beside her dead father and her dead brothers and sisters, all dead in the dark room, shot by Phalangists in the massacre at Tel Zaatar, would speak of death as it is. As would the Irish girl whose mother, brother and grandfather were all killed in separate, freakish incidents in the Troubles; and the eight-year-old Cambodian boy who buried his mother who had starved to death under Pol Pot; and the fifteen-year-old Vietnamese boy who was selected to be killed for food on a boat with a murderous captain; and the Lebanese boy whose testicles were blown off in an Israeli bombing raid and who now knows a different kind of death. They would all speak of death as devastation, and none would attempt to explain or excuse it.

These at least were the considered reasons for seeking the thoughts and feelings of children in war zones. There was one practical reason as well. Children are easy to talk to; they take every question at face value and usually respond directly to whatever is asked. One of the most unnerving discoveries on this journey, in fact, was that the children would answer almost any question that was put to them. No subject was too personal or painful. The shooting of a sister, the torture of a friend or of oneself; all such things, if inquired into, would—with the one exception of a Cambodian girl who would not speak to me of an incident she witnessed three years ago—be treated like questions about height, weight and age, and answered in calm, steady tones. This was not necessarily a sign of their comfort. The children who live with war know very well that adults can be terrifying people. They spoke when they were spoken to.

In the long run, however, none of these reasons, either practical or speculative, would have been sufficient to push me to travel twenty-five thousand miles on one leg of a journey and eleven thousand more on another in pursuit of questions that might never be answered. Nor would the love of danger, which did not at all burn in me before the trip, and does not now. If there was a central motivating force here, it resided in nothing objectively contemplated, but rather in a few visual images that are so strong I do not need to recall them.

The first was a television news picture of an Iraqi boy of three or four, standing alone and wailing in the rubble after an Iranian bombing raid of Baghdad in April 1981. The picture was on the screen for only an instant, yet as far as one could see, the boy was not crying out of physical pain but out of sudden and vast bewilderment. As soon as I saw him, another picture came to mind. This was the famous photograph taken during the American war in Viet Nam, of a Vietnamese girl, her clothing burned away by napalm, running toward the camera screaming terror and indictment.

The third image was also a picture, a drawing in a book done by atomic bomb survivors in Japan. The book is called *Unforgettable Fire*. Many of the pictures are so suffused with fire that one feels the hectic heat in the reds and yellows. But to me the memorable drawing was one in black and white, a greenish-black for the gate, and a gray-white for the child leaning against it. The gate led to a garden in Hiroshima. In the drawing the boy looks asleep, but as the artist explained in a caption: "When I approached and then touched him, I found that he was dead. To think that he might have been my own son made my heart ache."

23

It is my own son, my oldest child Carl, who carries the final image for me. Carl is sixteen today. The picture in my mind is of a time when he was four or so. He asked to come with me to park the car in a garage. I agreed. The evening was cool for August, and the city deserted. I was distracted with some problem, something I quite forget now, so I did not take notice as we began to walk to the car that Carl had not thought to wear a jacket. He did wear a hat, however, a white plastic nonsense that was supposed to be a racing driver's hat and that seemed two sizes too small for his head; it tottered there like a leaf. Self-absorbed, I was walking a bit ahead of him. Then absent-mindedly I turned and saw that he wore no jacket. No jacket in that weather? I roared with rage and ordered him to go back upstairs, that he could not come to the garage with his father because he wore no jacket.

At my eruption Carl looked forlorn, but only for an instant. Turning from me, in his white plastic hat, he walked back up the steps to the apartment house without a word of protest. I see him doing so at this moment. I rarely think of him, in fact, without seeing his back, the steps, my shame, or without considering how easy it is to abuse what we control.

To this image others, collected on the journey itself, have been added since, all bearing essentially the same cautionary message. They lie heaped around me now as I begin to try to piece the journey together again—all the fragments of material spread out in a false tidiness on several tables, one long desk, a bed with purple sheets, two chairs and a piano stool. Notes and pictures hang from a huge bulletin board, ten feet wide and five feet high, a godsend for the task of organization. I pace the large Victorian room I have sublet for the effort and scan these fragments like a movie sergeant inspecting recruits. Maps, itineraries, snapshots, newspaper clippings, a dozen legal-size note pads filled with my scrawl. On the long desk lies the color slide of a sculpture of a hand done by an Israeli girl in response to a PLO terrorist murder. Beside it a PLO badge, the gift of a fifteen-year-old boy who defended a stronghold in West Beirut.

Beside that a bright blue airplane drawn in crayon by a Cambodian boy. The plane was to take him to France.

Encircling a cassette tape recorder, fifty cassettes are arranged in piles by country on a brown chest of drawers. The high, soft voices of the children fill the room, all the languages eventually blending and sounding like one. Some cassettes play music: the songs of an Irish girls' chorus; a folk song performed by two Israeli boys; the children of a West Bank Palestinian kindergarten shout-singing "Pal-es-teen!" One cassette produces a Khmer folk dance in which the bare feet of the children can be heard keeping time with the wooden instruments, scuffling on a dirt floor half the world away.

All here, every scrap, memento, face and name. Hadara, Heather, Khu, Meng Mom, Elizabeth and Bernadette, Nimrod, Dror, Nop Narith, Ahmed the soldier, Nabil the tennis player, the brothers Trung and Ha, Hilda the flirtatious, the beautiful Waffa, the vengeful Joseph, Lara in her mourning, Thanh in his madness, the baby Palestine, and Keith the upstanding and Peov the tormented—all staring expectantly at the one who stares at them.

High on the bulletin board is pinned a letter from Nhon, the Vietnamese interpreter who met Trinh with me on the pontoon in Hong Kong, and who is now in California trying to secure an exit visa for his wife and boy in Saigon. The letter, penned in black ink with a perfect hand, was written when Nhon was still in Hong Kong. It gives news of the children we spoke with, and it says that Trinh and her mother are living in Kai Tak, one of the refugee camps, waiting to learn where they will be relocated. When the sun goes down here, it rises over Trinh. This is a good time of day to begin a journey, particularly when one proceeds eastward and there is a continual closing and opening of light. I began mine on September 14, 1981, flying from New York to Belfast, into the dark.

TWO

Belfast

The neighborhood, Pierce tells me, is called Divis Flats. The name confuses me, not accustomed to making the connection between "flats" and apartments. I picture the deserts in Nevada and peer into the dark, dead stone of the housing project, searching for the flats. Unable to read my mind, Pierce goes on talking. One of Bill Pierce's great gifts is that he always goes on talking; and while I regarded this logorrhea with dread and apprehension when we first met on the plane, I eventually realized that unlike most talkative people, Pierce knows not too little but too much. His brain teems with facts. On the subject of Northern Ireland he can talk for hours at a clip, which is exactly what he did flying over the Atlantic. Had not God equipped Pierce with a mellow radio announcer's voice, I would have stayed awake all night. Pierce, I believe, did so.

Not that he showed the smallest sign of fatigue when we finally arrived in Belfast. We changed planes in Dublin and flew north from there. That brief stop offered a moment of nostalgia for me. I was a student in Dublin in 1965. During the whole

27

year my wife and I lived there and in other parts of the Republic of Ireland, not once did we ever go north. Too dull, our friends assured us. No longer. Say "Ireland" to anyone these days, and all one pictures is Belfast, and possibly Londonderry, the dark northeast corner of the island, grown famous since the protest riots of 1969 as a world where people don odd black masks, toss petrol bombs, and starve themselves to bones. Pierce adores the place. He spent most of last summer here on assignment for *Time,* taking photos of the events related to the hunger strike of 1980, of the funerals and armored car burnings. He stayed on after that only because he wanted to. I think his sympathies lean toward the IRA, but he seems more generally sympathetic with the idea of struggle in the abstract, or perhaps, because he is a photographer, with the images of struggle. He is also the most gentle fellow imaginable, in spite of the fact that he affects the appearance of a hoary sixties brick thrower. Side by side, we look like Charles Manson and his parole officer.

We are side by side in Divis Flats, though for what purpose I cannot tell. Pierce could not wait to get out on the streets, so after dropping off our luggage at the Hotel Europa ("It's been bombed twenty-nine times!" Pierce exulted), we headed straight for this slum with nothing happening, no life in sight. This constitutes my introduction to Belfast. On a long gray wall is written fairly neatly: "Smash H-Block," that being the H-shaped section of the prison where the IRA prisoners are kept. Several windows show bullet holes. Others display black flags of mourning for the hunger strikers. Still others, large photographs of the strikers themselves. Rats skitter in huge gray pits, possibly sewage pits, that are soggy with rain. "Kids like to hunt them," says Pierce. My shoes crunch the glass chips covering the ground. I watch four young boys fling bottles down a huge piece of pipe jutting out from the earth. It looks like a giant's thimble. We too are being watched, by a cluster of teenagers, some furtive, some bold-faced, loitering beside a burnblackened car.

"The important thing is not to look British," says Pierce, who clearly does not. One is made aware at once of a central element of Belfast life, that the presence of the stranger is immediately noted and scrutinized, not merely by the slum kids but all over town. Within two days I will be meeting people, both children and school officials, who will tell me the purpose of my visit before I get a chance to tell them. "The kids won't start with us here," says Pierce, "because we look like American journalists. But in the Protestant areas they'll knife you for exactly the same reason." He rolls his eyes toward heaven.

"It isn't nearly as bad as it was or as it can be," Ed Curran tells us back at the Europa, where he has come to greet Pierce and me. Ed, a trim, alert man in his late thirties, is deputy editor of the Belfast *Telegraph*. He is also the Northern Ireland stringer for *Time*, indeed the whole bureau, and he has kindly prepared a list of schools for me to visit starting tomorrow: two Catholic, one Protestant. Ed himself is Protestant, born in Belfast, educated at Queen's University. Since the mid-seventies he has reported the Troubles for *Time* and the BBC as well as for his own paper. One can see why three large organizations rely on him. Explaining his reasons for recommending these three particular schools, he is careful to characterize the neighborhoods in which they are located, the likely backgrounds of the children, any important detail: Stella Maris is the school Bobby Sands attended.

There is sort of a post-Bobby Sands depression covering Belfast these days, Ed tells us. After Sands's death, there were others, and even now two young men are beginning to starve themselves to death in the prison the IRA men call Long Kesh and the Protestants, the Maze. Still, the hunger strike is withering as a political tactic. It is simply too hard on the families involved. In this Mrs. Thatcher will prevail. That leaves the war without a symbol for the moment, and this is a war that feeds on symbols. It is a gang war, a fight among neighborhoods and classes. When there are no full-scale riots, such as a hunger striker's funeral might occasion, the clashes take the form of kidnappings, booby traps, potshots in the night. Between these blips the city broods. Ed calmly recounts the history of its mayhem: Bloody Sunday, Bloody Monday, Bloody Friday, Mountbatten and the "death squads," the names and events by which his country has attracted the world's attention for a dozen years.

By the time the three of us part for the night, I am suffused with facts and terms for which I will be enormously grateful as I talk with the children. For them these incidents are part of common folklore; they will make shorthand references and I will not need to ask them to explain themselves too often. Pierce and I agree to go our separate ways during the week, I to keep a record of the children I meet so that Pierce can photograph them later on. Meanwhile, I will travel about the city on my own, aided immeasurably, as I soon discover, by a taxi driver, Joe McMahon, whom I hire the following morning. Joe is a chunky man with big hands, an innocent face and the bearing of someone in full control of his life. He will stay with me the week. Like Ed Curran, he appears to know everything about Belfast, everybody as well. We hardly drive three blocks without an oncoming car flashing its headlights at Joe's taxi, which signal Joe returns, a wink of mutual recognition.

The Cross and Passion Secondary School, all girls, is located in Andersonstown, described by both Joe and Ed as a rough Catholic area. The school building is situated next to a brewery, and the sidewalk out front bears burn marks where a car was set afire in a riot. Inside, all is composed and muted. Nuns shush the light chatter. The girls swish by and giggle in their green and yellow uniforms. Their heels click on the linoleum. On the wall of the principal's office is a Pope John Paul II calendar and a serene poster of a tree and a pond, on which is inscribed, "God is nearer to us than we are to ourselves." Through the windows I can see the brewery's high smokestack and the streaked sky slung low like a circus net. I remember those Irish skies. I remember the soft female Irish voices as well. That year in Ireland I lived in Connemara for a while, where the women gossip musically in Gaelic. The English has the same up-and-down tones.

Sister Marie Antonine gives me a gentle once-over through thick square glasses with black plastic rims. She looks kind but canny. The Virgin prays above her desk. She has two girls in mind who might interest me, and she will allow me to talk with them, but not without their parents' permission. She can get the Livingstones' OK right now, over the phone. I will have to return another day to speak with Elizabeth Crawford. I am told I must be careful with both girls. Elizabeth has had three deaths in her family in the past eight years, and Bernadette's sister Julie, fourteen, was killed only last May by a plastic bullet fired directly into her head from a British army Saracen. The Army uses plastic and rubber bullets to quell disturbances. In theory these bullets are to be fired at the ground so that they will hit only on ricochet. In practice they are often shot straight at their targets. Julie was killed in a protest demonstration involving mostly women.

Bernadette, fifteen, is a fifth-former in the Cross and Passion School. She sits by the window in Sister Marie's office and looks straight at me, holding her hands clasped below her green and yellow tie. From time to time, she brushes a wisp of quite blond hair from her eyes. The eyes are at once soft and stubborn. The delicacy of the hair is set against the flat pride of the face.

"One of the hunger strikers had just died, you know? Francis Hughes, I think it was. Yah, it was. And Julie and her friend had just come out of a shop. And there was the bangin' of the lids. [Garbage can lids; a signal of mourning and anger.] Suddenly people started running. And the army Saracens came down the road, you know? Six-wheeler Saracens? And Julie dove. But when her friend tried to pick her up, she couldn't move. She was still conscious on the way to the hospital. But she wasn't all there, like, when we left her. Mommy kept ringing the doctors all night to see how she was. The thing they were afraid of was the blood leakin' into her brain."

31

"Were you and Julie close?"

"No. All we did was fight. She was the youngest, you know? There were thirteen of us, and she got everything her own way. The rest of us couldn't understand it. Julie was very nervous, you know? Weepy like. She couldn't stand an argument in the house, being the youngest, I suppose." After a pause: "Now I'm the youngest."

Asked how her parents are taking Julie's death, she says: "My mother will never get over it. She had Julie late in life, you know? Me daddy doesn't express his feelings. I think that's worse, don't you? He used to do a bit of singing, but he doesn't sing so much anymore, you know?"

You don't know, of course, but this, as I learn, is the way most Belfast kids tell stories. Each statement of fact is turned up at the end, like a question. It isn't as if they are asking you anything that actually requires an answer. The statement carries the presumption that you probably already know what she had been telling you, that everyone is so close in the close city, all information is shared.

No, she does not bear ill feelings against the soldiers in the Saracens. No, she does not seek revenge. She points out that the British soldiers are not much older than herself. Bernadette does have a few Protestant friends, but it's a strain because of the neighborhood she lives in. The Livingstones are residents of Lenadoon, an area Joe shows me later, where Julie's death is memorialized by a white cross on a small green. The neighborhood is loud with graffiti: "Don't Let Them Die," "Touts Will Be Shot." Touts are informers. In bold white letters across the jerry-built walls is written "Welcome to Provoland," the word "Provo" like "Provie" being short for the Provisional IRA. In a sense, the Livingstones are a Provo family, since Bernadette's two older brothers, Patrick and Martin, are serving time in the H-Block. One of them is up for murder. But Bernadette seems to have her own politics: "I don't like what the IRA are doin'. Like shooting people. I don't support them because I know what death is like."

"Do you think of death a great deal?"

"Not my own. I think of Julie's death." Looking about the room, I ask if Julie's death weakened her trust in God. "You tend to pray more," she says.

"Is it faith or superstition?"

"Both." She looks surprised at her answer. "A bit of both." She says that this experience has made her feel suddenly much older, that her mother now speaks to her of things she never used to talk about before. The picture emerges of Mrs. Livingstone clinging to her now youngest daughter. "My mother needs so much company now. I can hardly get out, you know?" Julie had the habit of writing her name inside book covers about the house. Mrs. Livingstone breaks down whenever she opens one of those books. "Things like that bring it all back."

"Do you think of Julie yourself?"

"All the time. I pray to her. Not for her, to her. She's looking down, you know?" The girl stares out the window. "She's *everywhere.*"

By agreement with Sister Marie I will return to the Cross and Passion School to speak with the second girl, Elizabeth Crawford, at week's end. For the present Joe drives me to the Stella Maris School on the other side of town. The building is a brick and stucco series of afterthoughts that could pass for a bakery or a government depot. Stella Maris is unusual because it is a Catholic school located in a Protestant neighborhood. This is Bobby Sands's alma mater. I ask the headmaster, William Curran (no relation to Ed), if Sands's death had any effect on the children. Not much, he says. His assistant recalls that she once caught a couple of boys playing a game called "Bobby Sands," but that was about the extent of it. She and Curran make a list of boys and girls I might talk with. They both suggest Paul Rowe, urging me, as did Sister Marie with her girls, to be careful with the boy, since the incident is still painful to him.

The incident occurred on the night of May 8, 1974, when Frank Rowe, a forty-year-old bricklayer living at King's Moss

Road, Glengormley, Belfast, arose to answer a knocking at his door. He was immediately shot by a submachine gun fired either through the door or as soon as he opened it. Mr. Rowe was a Catholic married to a Protestant and lived in a Protestant neighborhood, which is why he was murdered. He had been warned. The night of the shooting his family was gathered in the living room. Mr. Rowe, his body filled with bullets, managed to get to his feet in the hall and escape through a side door so as to divert the gunmen from his wife and four children. He then staggered toward a neighbor's house across the road. The gunmen pursued and finished him off.

I ask Paul about other things first, about his bike riding, his soccer playing, his wanting to be a bricklayer like his father and his older brother. Paul is thirteen now. He was seven at the time of the shooting. He has a woman's face, still dimpled, along with the absolutely blue eyes of apparently all Belfast children, and brown hair parted carelessly down the middle; the sort of face the old masters sought. His school tie hangs cockeyed; it was knotted in a hurry. On the subject of his daily life, he describes it as solitary but not lonely. Like most of the city's children, he is not allowed to travel out of his neighborhood. "You get used to it." On the subject of his new five-speed racer, his eyes widen and his voice grows louder and higher.

But the tone drops steeply when I finally come around to his father's death. Dutifully he begins to relate the events, but he can only progress so far into the story, to the point where "Daddy, he ran to the back, to the next house," before he breaks down entirely and sobs. We wait. I try awkwardly to get him to talk of his feelings about his father's death today.

Joseph answers for him. His friend Joseph has accompanied Paul to the interview. They sit beside each other on low plastic chairs. Joseph is also thirteen. He has a small, tight head, a thin, clear voice, and he wants to grow up to join the Provies. "Revenge. That's what you want. Isn't it, Paul?"

Paul says nothing.

"Well, *I'd* want revenge," says Joseph, looking again to Paul.

Paul eventually nods. Then faintly, "Aye. Revenge."

As if to make his case forever, Joseph thrusts his face toward me. "*You*. You'd want revenge too, wouldn't you, mister?" Paul studies his feet. The conversation dissipates into chitchat about sports.

After I speak with a few other children in the school, I ask Curran if I may see Paul again, alone. Paul agrees. He sits beside me. Once more I stumble about on several subjects, but we both know I am really interested in one thing only.

"That business about revenge. Is that really what you want?" The boy looks suddenly self-assured. "No," he says. "It doesn't matter who done it. Nothin's worth killing someone."

As Joe starts to take me on my first tour of the city, I wonder if I am beginning to pick up a theme. I had done a fair amount of reading on the subject of Belfast children before I started on the journey, and practically everything indicated that the children of the city were hoods and thugs. Only one article, by Robert Coles in the *Atlantic*, gave the impression that there was a good deal of thoughtful variety in the children of Belfast. Otherwise, the newspaper accounts showed only bony, sinister young faces, butchered haircuts, eyes deep with nothing but destruction. They looked not at all like the children I had spoken with so far. Even little Joseph's fierce anger in his friend's behalf and his own dark ambitions seemed at least informed, not wanton. As for Bernadette, Paul and four or five others with whom I spoke in Stella Maris, they had no harsh words for Protestants in general, expressed not the slightest affection or admiration for the IRA as their defending army, and only spoke with enthusiasm about seeing the fighting stop. An Ulster policeman, killed by a sniper, was being buried that day. Catherine Steele, age twelve, offered only sorrow for the policeman's pregnant widow. "His baby will never know him."

It was far too soon to tell if this conciliatory attitude was general among the Catholic children and whether it extended to the Protestant children as well. Nor did I doubt the newspaper stories about the street thugs, since several of the teenagers I saw slinking among the crevices of Divis Flats looked exactly like the photographs I had seen back home. When I mention to Joe how gentle and peace-seeking the schoolchildren seemed, however, he is not surprised. He tells me of a nine-year-old boy he once caught stealing radios in the middle of the night. While driving the boy home to his mother, he delivered a stern lecture against crime, to which the boy paid no attention. Joe started to blow up at him, but then he saw that the child had fallen asleep with his head on Joe's leg. "Just a kid," says Joe. I am about to judge my companion an easy sentimentalist when he follows that story with one about two other kids who stole a car for a high-speed joy ride, both thieves so small that one steered the wheel while the other worked the pedals. Joe roars with laughter at that one.

We drive about the city once quickly, then cover the same ground more carefully, with Joe slowing or stopping by places that might interest me especially. The point he makes first is that Belfast is strictly divided among Protestant and Catholic neighborhoods, and each of these neighborhoods, some quite tiny, constitutes a pocket war zone of its own. I begin to grow familiar with the names: Ballymurphy, Sandy Row, Lenadoon, Turf Lodge, Ardoyne, Twinbrook, Rathcoole; the Catholic Falls Road area and the Protestant Shankill Road area. On Crumlin Road, which parallels the Shankill, there are four schools that sit across from each other, two Protestant, two Catholic. Every morning the children are escorted to their separate institutions by policemen carrying M1 rifles. At one time, says Joe, over a hundred army men in jeeps filled that street every afternoon. The trouble was that when the schools let out, the kids would start catcalling. Soon the parents would join in. In no time you had a major riot. All that is fixed today. The schools have staggered their closing times.

"O' course, there's one place where the Prods and Taigs are at peace." Joe grins and indicates the large Protestant and Catholic cemeteries that abut each other. "Yet space is hard to come by even there. The Catholics is spillin' over on the bogland. If you bury people in that, the coffins will pop out of the ground."

The city looks like a cage to me. It seems entirely enmeshed in wire, coiled and barbed, and supported by walls of corrugated iron, vast sheets of it, slabbed out in front of government buildings and other likely targets. The so-called Peace Line that separates the Falls Road from the Shankill is a masterwork of corrugated iron. It was erected by the Army. On the street itself are "dragon's teeth," huge squares of stone set out in uneven rows to prevent fast getaways. Downtown in the "control zone" no car may be parked unattended. Solitary figures sit like dolls behind the wheels, to prove there is no bomb. Around the corners the armored personnel carriers, called "pigs" by the children, lurch suddenly and poke their snouts, stopping to create instant roadblocks. Pedestrians are patted down by the RUC (Royal Ulster Constabulary) in the city's main shopping area. The Andersonstown police station, like a fly draped in a web, is barely visible behind a fence that resembles a baseball backstop. The fence is slanted inward at the top to fend off any rockets.

I ask Joe to show me a Protestant slum. The Shankill Road area looks more terrifying than its Catholic counterpart, perhaps because of the expectation that Protestants are supposed to be well off. I get out of the taxi and walk a block, patrolling the brown serried teeth of the terrace houses. A too sweet smoke hangs in the air like a gray underlayer of sky. Here, a hundred years ago, stood linen and flax-spinning factories. The terrace houses were originally built for the factory workers. There has been no work for years. Everyone is on the dole. Time has been given to the completion of small, patriotic projects. The curb stones are neatly painted red, white and blue, as are the bases of the lamp posts (in the Catholic neighborhoods these are done in green, white and orange). Red and white pennants that were strung across the road for the last July 12 celebration of the Battle of the Boyne are still aloft in September. Shaggy now, their color fading, they curl upward like a jack-o'-

lantern's smile. I am being watched blatantly. Men with stone faces glare at me from the doorway of a pub, the Berlin Arms, where earlier in the week a cache of machine guns was discovered under the counter.

I do not know it now, of course, but this one small block off Shankill Road is the only place I will feel personal fear on the entire journey. I will cringe at the bombing in Beirut on my second trip to Lebanon the following summer and be more than disconcerted by the gunfire there. But the Shankill has a menace all its own. Not because of the Berlin Arms or the machine guns or the eyes in the doorway. Nor because this is the one stop on my tour of the city where Joe refused to get out of his taxi, choosing rather to watch me from behind the wheel and to keep the motor running. But because here one could breathe the hate, feel it on his skin, taste the purity of it. Everything was dead in this place but hate. Back on the road Joe and I do not talk for a while.

Then I saw the mural, and I shout for Joe to stop. "That's somethin', isn't it?" he says. It is. There, fully covering a brick wall at least fifteen feet wide and twelve feet high, is a painting of a hunger striker lying in a bed, bearing a beatific look, the look of the suffering Jesus. He holds the rosary to his lips. Behind him is a representation of the H-Block, an enormous white H enclosed in gray walls. The entire background is black. To the left of the bed the figure of the Virgin approaches, bestowing her blessing. She is in white and blue, her head wreathed by a gray halo. Across the top of the mural stretches the legend "Blessed are those who hunger for justice." The calligraphy is exquisite, the whole work astonishing.

"The Provies don't have much use for the church," says Joe. "But they'll *make* use of her." Evidently. A billboard above the mural of the hunger striker carries an ad for chocolate bars. On we go, circling and recircling. Graffiti are everywhere. Protestant graffiti, praising England and "King Billy." Catholic graffiti: "Beware a risen people." Each area has its own. One writer at least shows a sense of humor. On a wall beneath the scrawl "No Pope in Ireland," somebody has written, "Lucky old Pope."

A girl with whom I spoke in Stella Maris said that the most important thing missing in her life was freedom. I begin to see why. It is not only that each neighborhood is a barricaded enclosure, but that all the neighborhoods, both Catholic and Protestant, look so much alike. Certainly the impoverished areas do. As we drive about we seem merely to be moving from one set of terrace houses to another, one series of doors to another. The doors are strangely elegant for the houses they lead to. I watch the people, particularly the women, enter those doors and close them tight. I feel a peculiar remorse at this, a low gloom that seems to come from somewhere outside me, but settles next to my heart nonetheless. I think the children know this gloom.

Do they realize how remarkably they resemble each other to an outsider, I wonder. Or have they so refined their differences that a Taig can tell a Prod a mile off? It occurs to me that I am observing a war between factions of a single people and that I will be doing so in other places of the journey as well. Cambodians fighting Cambodians; Lebanese, Lebanese; Vietnamese, Vietnamese. The Israeli Sephardim and their Arab enemies will not be so easy to tell apart at first glance. In some odd way, then, the wars I will be observing on this trip will all be family wars. This may account for their ferocity, their perseverance. It may account too for part of the sense of helplessness in the children.

At Joe's house that night I sit with his wife, Mary, their three children—Michelle, thirteen, Donal, ten, and Catherine, five—and Michelle's classmate Maire, who has come over to take a look at the American. Maire is black-haired, articulate, a highstrung Republican, though she, like the girl in Stella Maris, expresses pity for the recently slain policeman. We talk aimlessly around the fire. Catherine is mesmerized by the rotation of my tape recorder; it keeps her awake. Mary does counseling work with alcoholics. She says that drinking has gone way up in Belfast since the Troubles and that Catholic families are starting to fall apart for the first time in her memory. The older girls cite examples of dissolution in the families of their friends. Then they shift to the subject of the novels they are reading. Their favorites are by Joan Lingard. The novels concern the tribulations of Catholic Kevin and Protestant Sadie, who dare to fall in love in Belfast and strive to get married. Maire and Michelle agree; the best of the lot is *Across the Barricades*.

Finally, they talk of the nightmares they experience. Maire dreams of the sound of gunfire quite often. Donal says that he does too, and that he also dreams of being chased by gunmen and falling down. Michelle has a recurring nightmare of being trapped in a shop by a mob. As we grow sleepy Maire lays her arm casually on my knee and rests her head on top of it. I feel at home. Suddenly Joe remembers a joke about Paddy and Maggie McGuire. A terrorist tossed a bomb in their bedroom, you see, and the two of them were blown straight through the window. Joe feigns amazement. "It's the first time they've been out together in years!" The grown-ups laugh.

In the morning I gaze through the window of the Hotel Europa as the sun comes up reluctant behind thick bars of cloud. The street below wears a dull shine from last night's rain. I look over at one of the three hills surrounding the city, trying to imagine how Belfast looked when it thrived as a great clanging seaport, building ships, sailing them down the Belfast Lough for the world to admire. Now, rising above the iron and wire is modernity, drab gray-white office buildings stuck like headstones among the brown nineteenth-century houses. By 8 A.M. the city is in gear. The tiny cars scoot through the streets like dots in a tweed.

By nine I am standing in Ballymurphy, poking about on my own a bit before my appointment with the psychiatrist whom Ed Curran recommended as a source of information. Pierce and I conferred at breakfast, as we did every morning throughout the week. He attended the Ulster policeman's funeral yesterday and took a photo of a young girl standing in the procession, seen through the windows of the hearse. Pierce then sailed into a five-minute history of the petrol bomb, including an explanation of why the milk bottle is filled with both gasoline and diesel fuel ("makes it hard to extinguish") and why sugar and detergent are added ("helps it stick").

I stand in the ruins of the Ballymurphy playground. The grass is charred. The bottom poles have been yanked off the jungle gym. The slide is twisted and laden with rust; it looks like a scorched grasshopper. No child could possibly use it. There's a line from a poem by Seamus Heaney: "Is there life before death? That's chalked up in Ballymurphy." By 10 A.M. no one has as yet removed the dead brown cat curled up under the swings.

At the office of Dr. Alexander Lyons I ask if so drab and fierce an atmosphere can drive children crazy. "You have to understand," he says, "that in Northern Ireland the abnormal has become normal. Antisocial behavior is acceptable." He has gray-silver hair and a sleepy face. "The whole place, you might say, is emotionally disturbed.

"Of course, there is genuine insanity here as well." He remarks that among the various competing terrorist groups, the Protestants seem to draw more psychopaths. He describes the dread Butcher Gang, whose members he interviewed after the gang was caught. Joe also spoke of the "Butchers." The gang was so called because one of its leaders was a real butcher. They would drink all night, raid Catholic neighborhoods, snatch a victim off the street and mutilate him. By comparison, says Lyons, the murderous insanity of the IRA seems almost normal because of its putative political purpose. On the subject of children specifically, Lyons laments that "youth is used as a weapon here." He refers to the custom of positioning children on the front lines of protest demonstrations and funeral processions because the young lend moral authority to a cause. Yet the children survive it all. Lyons is far more impressed by their resilience than by their occasional breakdowns. A girl, a patient of his, who had three limbs blown off by a bomb, managed to hold onto her mind and eventually marry.

"Still, there is a legacy of hate in this country. And that's what worries me. In the long run [his voice is calm and certain], we are raising a generation of bigots."

If that is true, I have seen little evidence of it so far. It helps to remember, however, that I have been in Belfast a few days and Lyons a lifetime. I realize I must be quite careful taking my impressions, here and elsewhere, that I am flitting in and out of situations to which others have devoted years of study. I cannot yet tell the exceptions from the rules, and I may not be able to by the time I finish. Journalism is a philosophy of sorts, a journeyman's philosophy; one believes what one sees and changes his beliefs according to what he sees. As yet I have picked up no signs of a bigoted generation, but bigotry is not something people, children included, generally boast about. Lyons reminds me to take my time.

Still, I seem only to discover evidence of harmony in the children, even by accident. Shortly after noon, as I wait for Joe outside the Europa, a parade of children suddenly marches in a great clump past the hotel. There must be five hundred of them. They stop the traffic, the cars seem shocked. Placards are brandished and held aloft. "Ban the Bomb." "No More Hiroshimas." The group is called Schools Against the Bomb. They are joined by women pushing baby carriages, weaving purposefully among the marchers. "One, Two, Three, Four! We don't want a nuclear war! Five, Six, Seven, Eight. We don't want to radiate!" The demonstration moves by quickly. The children turn a corner, and the chanting dies away.

To this point I have spoken only with Catholic children. Later in the day I begin to find the same antiviolent attitudes on the other side, among the Protestants. Keith Fletcher is still stunned by the story of his Catholic friend whose father, like Paul's, was murdered in his own hallway. "They walked in, very polite. The mother didn't know what they wanted. She gave them tea. They drank it. When the father came home, they shot him."

Keith and Heather Douglas are both eighteen, in their final year at Methodist College, one of the largest secondary schools in Belfast, and a life removed from Stella Maris and the Cross and Passion. For one thing, "Methody," as the students know it, is mainly financed by the state and almost wholly Protestant. For another, it is pretty. The front gate opens on a semicircular drive; neat stone urns are filled with flowers; the archways whisper Church of England; and symmetry is mandatory. Across the road sits the great Queen's University, a mere expectation away.

At a long, dark wood table in the headmaster's office, Keith and Heather sit attentively like Ph.D. candidates, Keith in a navy-blue blazer and a blue and white tie, Heather wearing the same school tie but under a sweater with its sleeves rolled up to her elbows. Both students, I am told, are at the top of their class. Keith's jacket is decorated with three small badges for leadership and achievement. His face appears a work of pure logic. Heather seems a bit less organized, with her huge tinted glasses and infinite black curls.

"You have to really struggle to find the differences between the children," she says. "You can tell by the schools, of course, and by the names—Seamus versus Oliver and all that, and Long Kesh instead of the Maze. Then there's the *H* test. Have you heard of that one? I was playin' with some fellas in the park one day, and suddenly one of them stops me and makes me say the alphabet. So I go *A, B, C,* till I get to *H,* which I pronounce 'aich.' That's all right. It means I'm a Prod. But if I had said 'haich,' I'd have been a Taig." She laughs mockingly.

Asked if they think that any good can come from all this trouble, Keith says that it made him less bigoted, not more. "I think that the fact there was such polarization made you aware of the differences early on, made you examine what the differences really were. It led me to the conclusion that there

43

really wasn't much of a difference. Certainly not worth pola-rizin' about."

Heather adds that when she was much younger it was fun growing up in Northern Ireland, "kind of special. We played soldiers and terrorists, the way I suppose Israeli kids play Jews and Arabs." A few days later in Israel I find this to be so. The fun did not last long, she says. "Some people feel threatened by what others believe. They invent so many reasons to keep on fighting." Her voice sounds weary for a moment. "Too many people have too many reasons."

Both agree that there is no sense of authority in Northern Ireland, not in government, not in families. Keith is particularly disturbed by this. He says that one of the reasons he learned self-discipline at an early age is that he saw so little discipline around him. (Heather teases him, contends that Keith would be a stuffed shirt in any circumstance. Caught, Keith smiles and allows that it's so.) I suggest that there is not much respect for authority in other countries of the world either. But Heather in-sists that Northern Ireland is special. "There's no stability here at all." That is why she doubts she will live in her country as an adult. The children in the Stella Maris and Cross and Passion schools said much the same thing. Keith, who wants to become a zoo veterinarian, admits that part of him wants to live and work in Northern Ireland, but "because of the narrow-mind-edness and pettiness here, I'd have second thoughts."

Heather hopes to study theater at Cambridge University. She says the narrow-mindedness applies to all aspects of their lives. Her voice sounds both dismayed and bitter as she recalls having gone out with a Catholic boy for a while and the trouble every-one gave her.

I raise Dr. Lyons's prediction about a generation of bigots. Keith says it's possible, that "the hate can be so deep inside, you don't even know it." In his experience, however, the grown-ups are far more bigoted than the kids.

Heather concurs, vehemently. "You see"—she leans forward on the long table—"the society is so compressed. I feel a lot

44

closer to Catholics in Northern Ireland than I do to Protestants in England. The children have shared an experience here." She considers this. "We've shared a life."

Dining with the Currans that evening, I realize that in their lovely, stately house I am seeing an ideal consequence of the world of Methodist College. Ed himself went to Methody. His wife Romaine, a physical education teacher, is gracious, expansive. Their four small children descend the Victorian staircase for hugs and goodnights. Each is wrapped in his bathrobe like a piece of expensive candy. The neighborhood is called Malone. Most of the places are huge, have names, and are hidden by well-established trees and tall, thick hedges. The houses sit back from the quiet road like dignitaries at a parade. At dinner Ed tells me that the only complaint in Malone concerns the stink from the local offal factory. Still, the Currans talk of fear here too. A judge who lives across the road engages a full-time bodyguard. Romaine says, "At least the children are removed from the worst of it."

That turns out to be true only for a while. I talk with eight-year-old Jonathan Curran in his bed before he dozes off. So far, he has known nothing of the Troubles but the "big booms" he occasionally hears from down in the city. That afternoon he was visited by a new neighbor and playmate, seven-year-old Claire Bradford, who was thereafter to become Jonathan's friend. Three months later, Claire's father, the Rev. Robert Bradford, M.P., would be shot to death by the IRA in a suburban community center not far from the Currans' home. Mrs. Bradford tried to explain the death to Claire by saying that her daddy was talking with people up in heaven. Claire asked why that was necessary when there are so many people to talk with down here.

Before dozing off myself that night, I glance at two booklets I collected during the day's wanderings. The first is an anthology of children's writings published by a national teachers association. One section contains posters that children drew in a nationwide competition. A poster by Caroline O'Toole of St.

Mary's Primary School shows a brick wall with "U.D.A." (Ulster Defense Association) and "Provies" scrawled on it. In the center of the wall is a white square with the words: "They have their slogans. Let ours be Peace." In the section of the booklet containing poems is an anonymous work by a "pupil from a Belfast secondary school." It deals with a murder scene at a front door like the one Keith described, or the one involving Paul Rowe's father. Another poem by a "secondary school girl in Derry" begins, "There is a hollow somewhere, a big hollowness that needs filling." It ends, "Help us, our children and our children's children."

The second booklet was given me at the IRA press office, not far from Divis Flats. This was another caged structure, more like a catcher's mask than a backstop, with a steel fence clamped on the door. The booklet, entitled *Rubber and Plastic Bullets Kill and Maim,* contains pictures of those killed or wounded by the RUC or the British Army, with short descriptions of the incidents. One whole page is devoted to the story of Julie Livingstone, and another page to a photograph of Julie's face, which also occupies the booklet's front cover. Julie looks back at me with a dimpled, isn't-this-silly expression. Her smile is heartbreaking, as the IRA propagandists intend it to be. Even in death she is useful, I think. And then I do not think, staring only at her face. On the booklet's back cover is the picture of a child in an open coffin, enswathed in white satin, her eyes shut, her face bruised, her hands clasped on her stomach. I cannot tell if this too is Julie Livingstone.

The following morning is to be mine in the countryside. Joe has agreed to take me south by the sea to the fringe of the Mourne Mountains. He lustily sings the first few bars of "The Mountains of Mourne" to make sure I know where we're going. On the way out of the city Joe points out Stormont, a sudden Versailles, set a long way back from the road; once the seat of Ulster's parliament, now an administrative office building for the Cabinet. We pass a Kentucky Fried Chicken stand. I will spot similar American exports in every country on the journey, including Thailand, and find them funny, appalling and comforting all at once.

Within moments we are in real country. Dark green hedges make quilts of the fields. "They'll stay green all year round, you know." In the distance the hill sheep flock like gulls. I glimpse the sea from time to time. Joe tells me that if we headed north, we could see Scotland from the coast of Antrim. We both notice almost at once that there are no soldiers in sight. We pass ancient abbeys and towers half fallen where they stand. The scene reminds me of the south of Ireland, of County Wicklow and the decaying manor houses on the greens. "Desolate splendour," J. M. Synge called it, referring to the power the dying and the living take from each other, the way they clash silently for control of the world.

Waiting for the ferry at Strangford Lough, I watch the swans preen on the shore. The currents here are strong and treacherous; the ferry has to sidle into the dock. On the other side of the lake, I sight the foothills of the Mournes wearing dark gray clouds for caps. The grass looks velvet. The pasture land is so rich and various, says Joe, people can taste the milk and tell which county it came from. He recalls it was in this area, in County Down, that he and other Belfast children were evacuated during World War II. He explains that as a shipbuilding center during the war Belfast was a bombing target for the Germans. It strikes Joe suddenly that he too was a child of war. He recounts the long periods of separation from his parents when he and his friends were safe from danger. "War has found us at last," he says, half to himself.

Heading north again in a clockwise tour, we continue to see no police, no Army. All this safe quietude is Northern Ireland too. Just as I am thinking so, Joe indicates a spot on the road near narrow water where ten Englishmen were killed in an ambush in 1976. Old men bike here this morning. We pass a town called Bright and then approach a golf course off a winding, muddy path. This leads to Long Kesh, Joe says. All I can see at first are two white horses nuzzling in a field and a woman poking her front garden. Then suddenly the corrugated walls loom up on our left, topped with coiled and barbed wire. A jeep rumbles by carrying four baby-faced British soldiers sporting brand-new mustaches. I sight a lookout post. We are fourteen miles from the city. Joe offers to show me the best view of Belfast, from Belfast Castle on top of Cave Hill. I look past a circle of bright flowers on the castle lawn down into the center of town, which seems to be swirling in smoke like a doused fire, then out again toward Belfast Lough and the sea, whence we came.

In the afternoon I am scheduled to return to the Cross and Passion School to meet with Elizabeth Crawford. By this time, I feel I am about to be introduced to a celebrity, since all the children who have had tragedy befall them are well known in the city and are referred to frequently. Every time I have heard Elizabeth Crawford's name mentioned, the eyes of the speaker have veiled themselves and the voice gone doleful. I assume this is the way Elizabeth, Paul, Bernadette and others will be regarded for a long time, if not forever—as objects of pity, or of a kind of wonder, like a spectacle of suffering. A girl at Stella Maris recalled how beautiful a boy was Patrick Crawford, then blushed deeply to think that she was flirting with the dead.

Patrick was fifteen. He was very tall, wore his hair cut short and resembled a policeman. They say that is how he was shot by mistake. Dead too is Elizabeth's grandfather, who was run down by a car in what appeared to be a sectarian killing. And then there was Elizabeth's mother, killed mistakenly in a crossfire between the IRA and the Army.

"There were ten of us at the time—seven brothers, two sisters and myself. I can't really remember much about the happenin'. I was seven. My mother was out doin' the shoppin'. I was sittin' in a neighbor's house, and I seen my older sister being brought inside, and seen that she'd been cryin' and all. That was when we found out that Mother had been shot. And everybody kept tellin' us that she was going to be OK. Then later the doctor came in and he was tryin' to calm us down, and sayin' that she was dead and gone to heaven and all this here. Just before she

48

Belfast children in a funeral procession for a Catholic councilman, a victim in a sectarian killing.

Paul Rowe, whose father was shot to death in their Belfast home by Ulster terrorists.

A boy walks in front of a mural expressing support for the hunger strikes in Northern Ireland.

Photographs by Bill Pierce

Two children of a Palestinian family huddle together in the West Bank town of Ramallah.

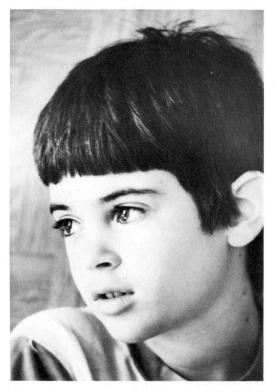

Nimrod, an Israeli boy at the Manara kibbutz, after reading a poem he wrote on the fear of abandonment.

A young Palestinian trains in guerrilla warfare at the refugee camp of Rashidieh in southern Lebanon.

Photographs by Eddie Adams

Eddie Adams

Lara, a Palestinian girl, at the head of a funeral procession for her parents, killed by a car bomb in West Beirut the day before.

died, me daddy had been talkin' to her. He was very upset, he was, though he's fairly settled now. When Mother died, we all found it hard to be close to him. He was always thinkin' of her —that's the way we seen it. I don't mean to criticize him. It's just that we were left aside, like, for a while. That was only a matter of weeks. After that we began to get close again."

Elizabeth sits in the Cross and Passion office where Bernadette was sitting earlier in the week. Her voice is quiet, her smile hesitant. Every feature is gentle—the way the long hair waves, the way the lidded eyes give solace. She may have the face of her mother.

"Did they ever find out who did the shooting?"

"The bullets in her body were from the IRA. They've got two fellas in jail for it now. My father works with their fathers in the brewery. He's quite friendly with them, actually. He just has pity for the ones who done it."

The man jailed for the killing of her grandfather was a member of the militant Ulster Volunteer Force.

"And Patrick? How was he killed?"

"It was a Catholic fella. They have him locked up too." All three, then, died in different parts of the violence. "When we were younger, we couldn't understand it. We didn't know where to turn or who to blame. We asked the adults, and the adults, they all had different views on it. I kept askin', Why is all this happenin' to *us?*"

I repeat the question I put to Bernadette. "Did it shake your belief in God?"

"Not in God. In man."

She goes on about her life: about cooking and cleaning for her father, about the occasional movie she gets to (*Friday the 13th*—"a good scare") and the occasional book (*Across the Barricades*). She suddenly seems invested with an ancient image. She is Ireland, this girl; not Northern Ireland, but the whole strange place, that western chip of Europe stuck out in the Atlantic with no natural resources but its poetic mind and a devouring loneliness. In peacetime that loneliness is intense but beautiful. In time of war it is merely intense. Here is Elizabeth at the window watching rain. Or Elizabeth shopping for groceries. Or Elizabeth walking home under that tumultuous blue-black sky. I could see it. Children often relish being alone, because alone is where they know themselves and where they dream. But thanks to the war, these Belfast children are alone in a different way. Elizabeth is not dreaming of what she will be. She looks about her and knows quite well what she will be, what her life and that of her children will be in that dread city. And like Keith and Heather, she wants out.

"Do you think that you could marry a Protestant boy?"

"If I find one nice enough. [A graceful laugh.] But if I ever did get married, I'd end up emigratin'. I would not want to live here, bringin' my own children up in the Troubles. 'Cause I was hurt. And I wouldn't want that to happen to them."

It is easy to picture Elizabeth as a parent, because she seems a parent already. Like Bernadette, she has been rushed into adulthood. Now she must take care of her father as if she were his parent—he who does not like to talk about the Troubles, or about the past, and who seems to have settled, quite justifiably, for a life of determined peace and quiet. He may never change. A grown-up parent sees life in stages, knows fairly well when a child will outgrow or overcome this and that. But how does a child-parent know the same about grown-ups? In a sense, more patience and understanding are asked of these children than of any real parent.

You wonder, in fact, if they begin to love their parents a little less for the multitude of responsibilities imposed on them. Or, for that matter, if they love them less for the danger they all are in. I remembered reading in Philippe Aries's *Centuries of Childhood* that in primitive worlds the high infant mortality rate inured parents against caring for their children too much because they knew they would probably lose them. Does the same obtain in places where there is a high parent mortality rate? Perhaps the children here begin to withhold some of their love from their parents as a pre-emptive strike against the assassins. It would be reasonable. It would be reasonable too if they loved them less simply for being grown-ups, for being partly responsible for the weeping in the streets. Yet they seemed to love their parents more, not less. They love them with greater caution, since whatever these children touch may explode or disappear. Still, when they spoke of their parents, it was with the most delicate mixture of faith, encouragement, pride, fear and regret. It was the way, in fact, one sometimes hears the parents of brain-damaged children speak of their young.

"Do you think that one side in the Troubles is more right than the other?"

"No," says Elizabeth, "neither is wrong. But they need somethin' to bring them together. I really don't know where fightin' gets anybody. It's only goin' to bring more dead, more sadness to the families."

She is told the story of Paul and Joseph in Stella Maris, of Joseph's urgings and of Paul's response.

"Don't *you* want revenge?" I ask.

She seems stunned by the question, and regards me with a look both pitying and severe. "Against whom?" she says.

On the way out of the building I stop by the art and music rooms. The art instructor shows me several dour self-portraits done by the girls, then pauses at a child's diorama of a wizened Raggedy Andy doll cradling a petrol bomb in its pink arms. Its socks are striped red and white, its shoes brown oxfords. The thing is clownish, manic. In the music room the girls' chorus is seated neatly in rows, about to rehearse a song from the musical *Joseph and the Amazing Technicolor Dreamcoat*. They clatter to their feet as I enter, and are amused by my embarrassment at their formality. Sister Marie invites them to go on as they were, and their teacher plays the introductory bars on an upright, filling the room with loud and hollow chords. Then the girls sing:

> I closed my eyes, drew back the curtain
> To see for certain what I thought I knew
> Far far away someone was weeping
> But the world was sleeping, any dream will do.

CHILDREN OF WAR

I wore my coat with golden lining
Bright colors shining, wonderful and new
And in the east the dawn was breaking
And the world was waking, any dream will do.

A crash of drums a flash of light
My golden cloak flew out of sight
The colors faded into darkness, I was left alone.

May I return to the beginning
The light is dimming and the dream is too
The world and I, we are still waiting
Still hesitating, any dream will do.

My last evening in Belfast I accompany Pierce to a children's carnival, one of several set up from time to time by the Youth Council of Belfast. I have already said regretful good-byes to Joe and Ed, realizing that the entire journey will include visits with people for whom I develop affection and whom I am unlikely ever to see again. Fortunately, it will be possible to reconvene with Pierce in New York, although that is not where we will work together next. At this moment in Belfast neither of us imagines that within the year we will be searching for children again, traipsing through the ruins of Beirut.

For the present our ground is the Beechmount carnival. Its mere existence serves as a reminder that as many forces as there are working against the children of this city, plenty of people are working for them. The gleaming new Andersonstown Leisure Center won a prize for being the best of its kind in the United Kingdom. Bernadette called it "gorgeous," and Elizabeth said she liked to play "the badminton" there and to disco in the Rollerama. Earlier in the day I even caught sight of an adult-organized cleanup going on in Divis Flats, grown-ups and children together in high spirits loading garbage bags with street trash and painting over the graffiti on the walls.

Now the carnival begins on a hill overlooking a playing field high above the city. A constable is shot in the back that night at about the same time, but no one at the carnival has heard of it yet. This is a time for play, for joyriding in the bumper cars and knocking about in the People Mover. The cool air roars with the Beatles' "You're Gonna Lose That Girl." Parents force smiles going down the three-story Superslide, while their kids take the thrill in stride. Down on the field, boys kick a soccer ball in what is left of the daylight. Pierce wanders among the rides, toting his cameras, and collecting a retinue of teenagers as he goes. I tag behind, trying to look as if I too am doing something.

"Do you come from New York?" asks Sinead Doherty, fifteen, who wants to be a beautician and sports a fancy hairdo for a start.

"I do," I tell her.

"Oh. I wouldn't go there. Murders everywhere."

By eight o'clock the sky is black, and the city pops on in a fluorescent amber. It has a noise, this city, like a train or a wail. Tonight the carnival's noise prevails. The place is packed, the faces glowing orange and red in the wild spinning lights. At the giant revolving swing a man solemnly takes tickets and the children mount the seats in pairs. Slowly the machine turns; slowly the nickelodeon starts up; and the chains that hold the swings grow taut until they parallel the ground. Suddenly the children are on their sides in the air, whirling above Belfast, impelled from the center by centrifugal force.

THREE

Israel

The Israel to which I traveled in September 1981 was a much different place from the Israel I was to see in the postscript to this journey, when I passed through the country on my way home from a devastated Lebanon in July 1982. In July Israel was in the midst of launching the most violent attacks in its history, and it was also the recipient of some of the most violent verbal attacks that the rest of the world had ever inflicted on it. The atmosphere within the country itself was defensive, arrogant, dismayed, bristling, determined, each in its turn. The elements of shame and outrage would be added later, the following September, after the massacres in the Palestinian camps in West Beirut. That previous September, however, Israel was so quiet as to seem almost languid. On the afternoon of my arrival I stood outside Ben Gurion Airport, sucking in the sudden tropical air. Summer. I had flown into summer. From then on, I realized, it would be summer until the end of the journey, that as I proceeded eastward from Israel and Lebanon to Thailand and then to Hong Kong, I would see the world in a single season.

Early the following morning, after spending the night in Jerusalem, I headed north in the company of the photographer Eddie Adams, who would be my companion in Israel and in Lebanon, and a young American named Robert Rosenberg. Robert is a stringer for *Time* and a reporter on the Jerusalem *Post*. He is also a poet, a historian, a comedian, a folklorist, an indefatigable tour guide, a diplomat, a politician and a remarkable translator of Hebrew. All these gifts are encased in a robust, six-foot body that seems to require no rest. Robert urged us to go north first, because there one was likely to find children who have suffered war directly, both terrorist attacks and the shelling by Katyusha rockets that the PLO launched from southern Lebanon. At the time of my visit in late September, the first and longest cease-fire negotiated by Presidential envoy Philip Habib was holding, but one could still see signs of war. Soldiers hitched rides on the highway and sat face to face in the backs of trucks. Green fields were stained brown where the rockets had seared them.

Robert points out the sights with devoted animation as we drive north. It is clear that he loves this country and that he has forged a place in it. The trees; he makes sure that Eddie and I notice them, that we appreciate the fact that they arose from a dust bowl. "These are post-'sixty-seven trees." Evergreen and eucalyptus. I ask him about the patriotism of Israeli children. He cites the West Bank as an issue that divides them. "The kids born in 1950 have more guilt," he says. "Those born after 1967 regard the West Bank as part of their own land." He observes that the occupation has been going on for a full fourteen years now, that in that time Israel has seen an economic boom of U.S. aid and money, and much housing and office construction, that cheap Arab labor has bolstered the economy, and that a general modernization and Westernization of the land has set in. In short, the occupation of the West Bank has been associated with the good life by Israeli children, some of whom, he says, can be more militant than Menachem Begin.

Then too, "Begin introduced the idea of fear into the country." Robert is no fan of Begin, thus the hyperbole, but he grasps the grounds of his appeal. He remarks that Begin's way of thinking may affect the children as well—"this talk that every woman and infant will be in the sights of an Arab gun." The point is that such a thing is possible, even likely; Begin derives his political strength from the fact that Israel's enemies are real. Before we passed Haifa ("What a view from that city!"), Robert pointed to the site of the coastal road massacre, where in March 1978 eleven terrorists, having landed by boat north of kibbutz Ma'agan Mikh'el, proceeded to kill thirty-seven people and to wound seventy-six others by shooting individuals and opening fire on buses and cars, until they themselves were killed or captured. If there is no massive peace movement among Israeli children, Robert remarks, such incidents are the reason.

It was in the northern Galilee town of Qiryat Shemona, in April 1974, that eight children were murdered by three terrorists of the Popular Front for the Liberation of Palestine (PFLP), who had crossed from Lebanon into Israel before attacking an apartment house. One month later in the northern town of Ma'alot, three Arab terrorists held eighty-five children hostage in a schoolhouse; when Israeli troops stormed the building sixteen children died in the shooting. Two teenagers were killed by a bomb planted in a garbage bin in Tiberias in May 1979; in Beirut the PLO claimed responsibility for the bombing. In April 1980 five terrorists attacked the northern kibbutz Misgav Am, holding six children hostage in a nursery and killing two adults and a three-year-old before the building was retaken. The recollection of such events also serves to keep the feeling of war alive in the area.

But none of these incidents had quite the effect, either locally or nationally, of the attack on Nahariya that occurred in April 1979. One evening four PFLP terrorists entered Nahariya from the sea in a motor-powered dinghy, and after a brief aimless search for victims, came upon a four-story apartment house.

There they broke into the home of Danny and Semadar Haran, the young parents of two daughters, Einat, five, and Yael, two. They took Danny and Einat back to their dinghy on the beach. Danny they shot to death. And when the Israeli forces approached, one of the terrorists picked up the girl Einat by the feet and cracked open her head on a rock.

The daughter Yael died differently. When the terrorists burst in on their apartment, Yael and her mother were in a utility room, where they remained in hiding. Yael started to cry. In order to keep her quiet, Semadar clamped her hand over the two-year-old's mouth, very hard, so hard in fact that she inadvertently suffocated her own child. When the story became known, it drove the entire nation into a profound mourning. There was Israel's history in a single episode: the nation continually at war; the nation as mother protecting her children; the nation unwittingly suffocating her children for the wars in which she is caught.

This story is related to us by Zion Ben-Eli, a child psychologist in his mid-thirties who has worked with the children of Nahariya for the past four years. He has patient, reasonable eyes, a younger version of Dr. Lyons in Belfast. He sits across the table in a roadside diner where the four of us are the sole customers. The only other person in sight is the diner's owner, an excessively good-humored man who for reasons of his own has taken the occasion of our late lunch to try out several old jokes. Zion talks quietly against a background of forks clinking on plates.

He manages the Educational Psychology Station of Nahariya and is thus responsible for overseeing some thirty thousand schoolchildren, ages five to sixteen, in the area. After the attack on the Harans, he says, a panic overwhelmed the entire town. Children refused to do schoolwork. They reported headaches and nausea. For weeks they were afraid to leave their houses. Zion and his staff encouraged them to discuss their worries openly, both through art and conversation. There was also the matter of Semadar, the dead children's mother. People in the town did not know what to say to her. Zion worked with Semadar as well. She is now remarried and has another child, but understandably her recovery took a good deal longer than that of the town's children.

"In the beginning the children identified with the terrorists."

"Because they are exciting?"

"No. Because they are strong. And they seem to be omniscient. But this was a short stage. After a while they forget it. Adults retain the memories longer. Children are stronger than adults in these things."

He is asked if hardships themselves ever give strength to children. "That is a myth," he says. "Children work like fishermen. They cast about for models, taking something useful from everyone in the process." Do the children cast about for a model Israel? Do they ever discuss this? "Small people speak about small worlds," says Zion.

In spite of all the obvious penalties, Zion can see some good coming from Israel's wars. Yet he sounds more speculative than optimistic. "The people of Nahariya faced up very well to stress. The morality of the town improved afterwards. [I ask Robert if he means "morale," but "morality" is what Zion intended.] When you have something hard to face, and you face it, you come out better. I was also a child of war. I don't think that it damaged my personality. Nor did it affect my desire to remain in Israel. A war may bring people together."

He pursues this theme on the way back to his office. We drive through neighborhoods that were shelled, but there is nothing but suburban quiet now. The Educational Psychology Station is an adobe house with blue shutters and much of the paint peeled off. A tall, extravagant tree stands over it. Zion goes through a pile of papers until he comes up with what he wants: a mimeographed booklet of poems written by Nahariya children after the killings of Danny, Einat and Yael Haran. Robert translates the poems silently to himself, then reads

59

aloud, first in Hebrew, then in English, a poem that he finds
particularly impressive:

> If there's a God
> and yes, many claim there is,
> then how does it happen
> that little kids get killed?
>
> How is it that
> a girl who didn't even know
> what a gunshot is
> was killed by terrorists?
> And who knows if that was with God's help?
>
> How is it that
> everybody could be sleeping sound
> little Yael, a bigger Einat,
> Danny with Semadar,
> wonderfully,
>
> when suddenly, for no reason,
> just matter-of-factly
> they were shot to death?
>
> And how is it that
> the children
> who had not even yet managed to do anything
>   in their lives
> are the ones to be shot and the ones to die?
> Yet there still are those who claim
> that there is a God.
>
> If there is a God
> then how does this happen?
> Who even needs it?
> Let's get it over with.
> Let's finish this matter.

If there is a God
and yes, many claim there is,
then how does it happen
that little kids get killed?

The poem is by Hadara Minster, now a girl of fifteen, who
was twelve when the terrorist attack occurred. Hadara was the
Harans' baby-sitter, and she was very close to the family. After
the incident, Zion tells us, she refused to talk with anyone. She
would not go to school; eventually she would not leave her
home. Then Zion began to work with her. And one day—he
relates this with evident amazement—she simply pulled herself
out of her inertia by organizing a peace conference between
Arab and Jewish children in her school. She called her conference "To Bring the Hearts Closer."

As Zion tells this story, he begins to display pictures, like the
poems, that the town's children produced in order to clarify
their responses to the killings. One is of a blackened sky with a
small penciled flower on it. Two others are of disembodied
hands knocking at a door, presumably the door to the Haran
apartment. There is a drawing of a baby in a dinghy; another of
a solitary canoelike boat floating empty on placid water; yet another of four children facing backward in a boat that is on its
way to Lebanon. Other drawings are more violent: the face of
a terrorist spotted with blood, baring his teeth in a grin; Israeli
helicopters and submarines to the rescue; pictures of terrorists
captioned "Company" and "It is your end" (the terrorists re-
portedly spoke English). A drawing of a storm is entitled "The
People of Israel Alone in the Struggle." The most elaborate of
the drawings shows three segments in which the children of the
town are taking revenge on the terrorists, tossing bombs at
them, setting them afire, and finally mowing down those who
are left. There is also a lovely, melancholy sketch of daisies with
their heads bent. This one is called "An Imperfect Flower."

Then Zion produces a color slide of a work of sculpture entitled "The Hand of Fate." The hand is dark green, nearly black,

61

outlined in white, with watery blue streaks running along the index finger. It looks more like a bay than a hand, and may in fact be meant to combine the hands of the terrorists with the sea that the dinghy arrived on. This, too, is the work of Hadara Minster. She inscribed her sculpture to the memory of the father, Danny. Above the inscription she wrote in four short lines: "And in their death they commanded us to live."

Hadara lives just down the road from Zion's office. At our request she rides over on her bike. She has black hair and blue eyes the color of Elizabeth's in Belfast, but Hadara's hair is cut short, making the face look more forceful. It is one of those faces that seem absolutely feminine on a woman and absolutely masculine on a man. Her teeth show a gap when she smiles. She parks her bike on Zion's front lawn, and sits cross-legged beside it, in cutoff jeans. Her voice is gentle but clear.

"At first I didn't want to accept it [the killings]. I didn't understand how there could be such a thing happening to children. But afterwards I realized that even this was part of life. It made me sad to think that, in the beginning. But now I see things clearer than before. Not so emotional." Robert helps her find the word "emotional" and only a few other words; generally her English is good. She flattens her *o*'s, like a South African. "Now I am trying to look at things the way others do."

Asked if she means that she has come to see murder as a normal part of war, she says, "Yes, of course." I ask her then if she would also commit murder in a war. "No. The attack on that family was a different kind of war."

"And the Israeli bombing of Beirut last summer. Is that not also a different kind of war?" (In reference to the air raids of the summer of 1981.)

"Yes. I think it's terrible. We are behaving like terrorists. The children did nothing to us."

She automatically focuses on children whenever she mentions the victims of war. Many of the Belfast children did the same, as would the Palestinian and Lebanese children later in the journey. It is not as if they are simply naming their own

62

kind and complaining of their peril selfishly. Only that they, like adults, associate childhood with innocence and thus cite the example of the most blameless targets in order to make a point dramatically. Curiously, however, they do not include women in their expressions of sympathy, as in the phrase "innocent women and children." I doubt they think women less innocent. More likely, they simply know what it is like to be a child in pain or in danger, and in a sense they reach out to themselves. At one point Hadara described her relationship to the killing of the Haran girls: "I didn't see the murders, but I could feel them." She was not asked if she had seen the murders, since I knew that she had not. But she wanted to explain why they made so deep an impression on her. She actually felt the deaths of those other children.

"In the first days I couldn't even watch the Arab news on television. I certainly couldn't look an Arab in the face. I thought, All Arabs are murderers. It was the first time that I hated so much. I didn't like to hate, but I did so." She then explains how she expunged her hatred by participating in the peace conference that Zion described. She does not, however, mention that the conference was her idea. When I do, she acknowledges the fact with a nod and a brief *ken* (yes) but dismisses her initiative as unimportant. What bothers Hadara is that the conference did not work.

"No. It ended in anger. After the first meeting I asked, Do you think that to kill people is right? And all the Arab children said yes. I turned away from them. We didn't say good-bye." She pauses. "They told me this to my *face*." She raises her voice. Clearly she feels some special repulsion in that fact.

She considers the question of whether a second try might be worthwhile. "I think I'm ready for it again. Now I know what the Arabs really think, what they will say to our face. I won't be so horrified." Her response accords with the kind of world she says that she would ideally want to live in. "I would like people to have more patience. They must learn to listen. Maybe they mean the same things, but they don't always use the same words. Do you understand?"

When Hadara grows up, she hopes to be a social worker in Nahariya, to work particularly with children. She says she is still afraid that something like the Haran killings will happen in Nahariya again. "But this time I think I will be stronger. I must see the reality of it." Does she hold anyone responsible for such a state of affairs? "Yes. I blame adults. I blame them that small children grow up with this hate." Before departing, she poses for a picture, smiling on request beside a tree.

Eddie, Robert and I drive to the northern outpost of Metulla as the sun goes orange. The country feels sweet and empty at this hour, like New Hampshire on a late spring afternoon. Black goats feed on scrub near the highway. Robert points out Ma'alot, where the school was attacked, a pile of white shining blocks in the distance. To the left Crusader ruins; to the right the Golan Heights. "The Syrian artillery sat up there and shelled the valley below." The road is steep here; you honk at every curve. Over there are tank traps, Robert says. And there lies the fertile Hula Valley beneath us, a swamp in 1905. "A population was nearly destroyed in the process of drying up that swamp. One out of ten survived. Yet they did it!" By the time we reach Metulla, Robert has made sure that no carrot row or orange grove is passed without comment. His pleasure is catching.

From Metulla, Lebanon is clearly visible across a wire gate. Something is burning in a field a few hundred yards away; it is not a rocket. Here Christian Lebanese laborers park their cars when they cross over into Israel to go to work. A rose bush flourishes near two parallel fences. On a stone wall is carved the swords-and-ploughshares passage from Isaiah in Arabic, Hebrew and English. The flags of Israel and Lebanon flap side by side on blue and white poles. A recording of Ella Fitzgerald singing "Summertime" plays on a car radio. Soldiers from both sides patrol the border lethargically. This is a strange little spot for history. The hills turn lavender in the sunset. They merge with the sky, which is also lavender now.

I am suddenly aware that the deep fear I originally felt in going to Israel has abated considerably. The fear was based on the fact that during my first and only other visit to that country seven years earlier, my father died in New York. I learned of his heart attack as soon as I arrived in Tel Aviv, and booked passage on the first return flight, which left on Saturday, the Sabbath, and was therefore officially unscheduled. On the way home I sat among half a dozen passengers dispersed in the huge jet and prayed for my father's recovery, though I felt certain he was already dead. When we got to New York, the plane could not land because a thick white fog lay over the airport. Contemplating this second trip to Israel, then, I thought of the fog, of the flight that did not exist, of the fact that I could not get down to my father. And I was afraid of some new disaster.

But both the purpose of this journey and the beauty of the countryside are expelling my superstition. As we drive south from Metulla, I watch the sky go from lavender to purple and then to a true black. As it does, the lights of the hilltop towns grow steadily brighter until they gleam like bracelets suspended in the dark. It is hard to think of this place as somebody's target, much less as an omen of bad luck. The car moves like a paintbrush through the landscape. The world feels absolutely still.

At night we visit a family in Qiryat Shemona. Their apartment is white-walled and modern; it might be anywhere in an American city. The grown-ups loiter in the kitchen as I talk with Daphna and Semadar. They are Hadara's age but chattier; often one girl doesn't complete a sentence before the other hustles in. Semadar is dark-skinned, with dark brown eyes and long dark hair. Her English is quite good. Daphna speaks only in Hebrew. She is lanky, wears white shorts and a bright pink jersey. Her eyeglasses make her look oddly attractive, like a sexy accountant. Both girls talk frantically with their hands, which seem at times to take off without them.

Semadar's parents want to leave Qiryat Shemona, but to Semadar this is home: "I have roots here." She is still afraid, however. When the Katyusha rockets were falling, Daphna imagined that she could see the faces of the enemy. "They have terrible eyes. Oh, terrible! And mustaches!" (I maliciously point out that Robert also has a mustache; we agree that he is terrifying as well.) Asked if she can visualize a girl like herself in Beirut picturing the same sort of thing from the opposing perspective, Daphna admits the possibility but without conviction. "They want to kill *individuals*. They want to come after us *personally*." Semadar is a bit more conciliatory: "Both sides suffer."

Her mother Leah is a psychologist like Zion. She works with teachers in Qiryat Shemona. Standing behind the girls now, having been drawn from the kitchen by their conversation, she offers the opinion that the continual tension may have shaped the thinking of the town's children. "People don't speak about the stress, but they are exhausted by it." Leah's brown hair is graying. She has large, weary blue eyes, a face on which sadness is beautiful. Daphna confirms that there is tension. She notes that there are no ordinary acceptable noises in Qiryat Shemona; every door slam and backfire brings a gasp. Her family keeps the lid on, she says. She is even forbidden to yell at her brother. "Everyone is always calming everyone else. I wonder if children really ought to be brought up in these situations."

Semadar chips in suddenly: "Everybody's right and everybody's wrong at the same time. I know the terrorists are evil. But, on the other hand, they wanted a state. And I don't know if we should think like them, but we *also* wanted a state. And we were ready to kill for it." Daphna: "Sometimes I hate all Arabs." Semadar, changing her tune: "Sometimes I think that if I could, I would drop them all into the sea."

"Do you think that you could ever fall in love with an Arab boy?"

Both at once: "Are you *crazy!*"

66

Semadar: "I hate them without reason. In order to preserve my sense of self, I have to hate them." For the first time in the evening, no one talks.

Leah is visibly disturbed by what she hears. She had not dreamed that the girls were so angry and adamant. Taking a clinical tone, she cites the connection between hate and fear: "When you cease to be frightened, you cease to hate." Nonetheless, she says: "I am shocked by the hatred of these children. My daughter's hate." Leah is a Sabra; she grew up among Arabs. "I was never taught to hate them, not like this." The girls listen to her silently without offering demurrers that might soften their position. They do concede that not all their friends feel as they do.

As if talking to herself, Leah concludes wistfully: "It's very bad that my children never learned to speak Arabic. Ignorance is the beginning of suspicion." The evening ends politely over coffee and light chatter.

It is important to realize, Robert tells me afterward, that the children of Qiryat Shemona are likely to be less tolerant than those elsewhere. One reason may be that last summer the citizens of Qiryat Shemona evacuated the town during a heavy shelling. This is a thing not done in Israel; it smacks of cowardice or at best a lack of proper resolve. The hatred of the children may thus be tied in some way to a general defensiveness, a form of shame. Robert also contends, by no way of apology, that Daphna and Semadar are not typical in any case, which the girls themselves confirmed. On so brief a visit minority and majority tendencies are impossible to ascertain. One thing is evident, however, in an on-the-run comparison of Irish and Israeli kids; that the Israeli children, unlike the children of Belfast, do not form their views of war solely on the grounds of personal experience and personal morality. Sophisticated or not, they all have an articulate sense of Israel's nationhood and Israel's politics. Whatever confusions they voice seem to arise from their awareness that they are Israelis as well as kids.

To the center of Israeli nationhood, then, to a kibbutz, we

proceed the following morning, Saturday. We start out quite early, observing the green-and-brown-patched hills in the hazy light. The fish ponds glow like polished slate. On the road we pass a group of teenagers on a *tiul,* a day trip. They have come from the kibbutz at Manara, where we are headed. We stop to take in the view from high up. This is the route taken by the Israeli tanks on their way to capture the Golan Heights in 1967, and this spot, says Robert, is where the shells fly over on their arcs from Lebanon.

Two men were killed by a Katyusha rocket in 1978 as they walked past a wall in the Manara kibbutz. There is a hole in the wall, like a bite mark, where they were hit. It is the only sign of destruction in Manara, where everything else seems to flourish. Red flowers shine in dark green bushes. Babies in colorful sun hats waddle in the playground. The older children use the pool, an enormous rectangle of the purest blue carved into a ledge of terraced land below the playground. From the far side of the ledge, one may look down into a valley full of plums and avocados.

Dror and Nimrod, both ten, are the best of friends and share a bedroom in the kibbutz. Dror wears glasses and looks professorial. Nimrod has a dreamer's face. His brown bangs are cut evenly like a monk's over a pair of eyes the same shade of brown. The boys' room is spare, full of sunlight, and, like most boys' rooms, ridiculous. On the wall hang pictures of two white kittens, a deer, Popeye and Olive Oyl, and an El Al jet. The boys have done some pictures of their own. Dror displays a drawing of Begin and Anwar Sadat, both saying in a balloon above their heads, "Peace is going to come." Nimrod presents a drawing of Indian tepees. Why Indians?

"After the Jews they are the people I love most." He talks in a smoky whisper. "First, because the white men came and made them suffer, and they didn't deserve that. Second, I love how brave they are. I sympathize with them." Asked if his sympathies go toward all oppressed peoples, he says yes, "if they are innocent and are not against us."

Asked specifically about the Palestinians, he answers that he is still trying to make up his mind about which side is right: "Recently, when there was the shelling of Qiryat Shemona, and they showed the damage done by the Israeli planes in Lebanon, I looked at this and I said: 'Despite everything, I feel sorry that this is happening, happening by people to people. It is not like some animal is doing this.' When we first heard that there was retaliation, all the kids, me included, jumped up and cheered. Later I thought, What good is this revenge?"

Dror adds that he and his friends think a good deal about the children in Lebanon. "I feel terrible for them. They don't have as good shelters as we." He often wonders if they have the same toys and games. "If peace should ever happen, perhaps it would be possible to play with them."

Asked if there is such a thing as a good war, both boys say yes. "Among kids there are good wars. Take the other day. We found a big crate on the lawn, and we played king of the mountain with it. That was a good war." They recreate their excitement, recalling the game. They are asked if they see an analogy between playing king of the mountain and an adult war over territory. Dror says that playing with that crate reminded him of a war. "Even a game can wind up in real tears." They will not speculate whether such games lead to grown-ups' wars. Instead, they describe a different war game of their own, which they play with the children in another building of the kibbutz. They use military tactics. They take prisoners. The game is played according to the strictest rules.

"But the big kids break the rules!" They work up a protest on the spot and encourage each other's indignation. "They lose control! They tie our arms and legs to trees!" When it is suggested that real wars are often won by those who break the rules, Dror confesses that he occasionally breaks the rules himself, but that he feels bad about it. Nimrod says, "I will only break a rule when I'm in danger."

Lately, Dror has been writing poems, mostly about death. "I like poems that make you cry." His father, Moshe, who has been standing quietly near the end of his son's bed throughout our conversation, recalls that one day he found Dror crying over one of his own compositions. "He was just sitting there and writing something. He was so sad, he started to weep." Moshe chuckles to conceal his pride.

Nimrod writes poems about loneliness, which he keeps in a secret drawer. Sometimes he writes about Israel's loneliness, as if the country were "a little speck of sand alone in the world, with only a few other specks of sand who care about it." He has been rummaging for a poem he wrote about being abandoned. As he reads it aloud you can hear the internal rhymes in the Hebrew. Robert is exceedingly careful with the translation:

> I stood in front of a streetlamp
> without moving an eyelid,
> without even thinking
> And a small tear began to slip
> And fall into the ground.
> I swallowed my saliva with a deep breath,
> And I said: This is a difficult departure.
>
> I stood in front of a streetlamp
> without moving an eyelid,
> and without even thinking:
> Will it be bad or will it be good?

Nimrod is quite still after reading his poem. We watch him think about it again, looking into it. Would he write a poem about abandonment if his country were not always at war? Perhaps. Abandonment is not a fear limited to war. Yet it seems likely that an atmosphere of threat has brought that poem to the surface, just as it has brought Dror's poems about death to the surface, that in spite of the sunny florid world of the kibbutz, real specters visit these children. The novelist Amos Oz once wrote a short story called "Where the Jackals Howl," in which jackals that prowl the outskirts of a kibbutz serve as

70

symbols of several types of menace: Israel's present enemies, Israel's past enemies and the enemy of the haunted mind. These northern kibbutzim are vulnerable to a great deal, including the fearful imagination. Dror and Nimrod could not have failed to hear what happened to Yael and Einat, only a few miles away. Having heard, might they not wonder when a terrorist might be coming over the sea at night for them?

Then too there is the matter of death itself, apart from fear, particularly the death of children. When a child dies, he remains a child forever in the mind, a small, lively ghost. The war zones of the world are full of such ghosts—the Haran girls here, Julie Livingstone in Belfast—preserved in the local memory as terrible contradictions of terms: dead children. The grown-ups feel their presence as a plea, accusation or heartbreak. But the children feel it differently. The dead share their territory, customs and desires. They have continuous transactions with the living. Perhaps this is why Dror and Nimrod seem cheerful one moment, brooding the next.

If a shelling of the kibbutz occurs at night, a nanny leads the children to a special shelter, below ground level, which is connected to the building. The parents have their own assigned places and duties. The children's shelter is cool, even at noon. Eighteen bunk beds, in tiers of three, line the antiseptic white walls, from which an intercom phone protrudes. The place has the clean and claustrophobic feel of a submarine. A door like a bank vault's is the only way in or out. Near the ceiling is an air fan and filter system, in case of gas attacks. Robert calls our attention to the fact that people who survived the death camps built these safeguards.

The time the two Manara men were killed near the wall, Dror and Nimrod felt the tremors of the rocket in this shelter. They, and some other children who have gathered around, proceed to imitate the sound of a falling Katyusha, Dror doing the rush of wind, Nimrod the squeaky flute. All at once, the children mount the bunks and break into a pillow fight. One mimics the absent nanny, telling them all to pipe down or else.

71

They have been forced to stay in this shelter for as long as two weeks at a stretch. A small boy watches this all intently. Eventually he musters the courage to ask me the question that has been bursting inside him: Do I know Dr. J or Kareem Abdul Jabbar?

In a music room Dror and Nimrod are about to sing a song, reluctantly. They have agreed to perform not explicitly in exchange for our doing them a favor, but they asked for the favor first. That night an Ecuadorian choir is to entertain at Manara, and the children of the kibbutz have been barred. The boys protest this act of discrimination, and seek our intercession on their behalf, which is readily granted. Now Nimrod sits at an upright piano, and the two of them sing a folk song similar to the American "Oh! Susanna." Their not-yet-changed voices sound exactly alike: "Don't worry, Shoshana / Someone is coming for you / Across the stormy sea / I am coming for you."

On the road back to Jerusalem I ask Robert what makes boys like Dror and Nimrod so different from the girls in Qiryat Shemona, and from Hadara too, though their sentiments were akin to hers. He allows for the obvious first: These two gifted boys would not be ordinary in any context and are bound to be considered special among their Manara friends as well. Beyond that, Robert ventures the opinion that the kibbutz experience itself may broaden one's tolerance and capacity for sympathy, that more of life is understood in a place where individual sacrifice for the collective good is the standard of living. He notes that both boys are religious, whereas many Israeli children are not. (Daphna and Semadar described themselves as atheists.) I take in Robert's view, but I have no way to judge it.

Yet it seems just as likely that the meanest impulses might also thrive in such a place, or worse, that one's exaggerated pride in self-sufficiency might lead to the most virulent and threatening contempt for the weaker breeds. All the lofty talk of special purpose and special will that attended the founding of the original kibbutzim must, in some quarters, have disintegrated into the cheapest sort of chest beating. Besides, the primary allegiance to the welfare of the group as a whole must play havoc at times with one's desire, and need, to show individual weakness and individual fright. A child who is afraid to show fear would surely be afraid to show affection. So would the theory go.

But this conjecture hardly applied to Dror and Nimrod. They seemed only enhanced by their participation in a highly structured world. Survival in a state of war also requires a highly structured world. I wondered, then, if these kibbutz children responded to war so admirably because they are familiar with its conditions—self-discipline, uniformity, esprit de corps, self-denial. In their ordinary lives they seem to know the best elements of war without paying the ultimate price for the enterprise, without killing. In a way, they may appreciate the institution not only because they are so well prepared for it, but because war shows them at their best, oddly justifying a particular kind of existence. This notion would build into a more general question as the journey progressed and would come to a head with the Palestinian children in Lebanon; but for the moment it simply occurred to me that everything about war might not necessarily be destructive for children. Under some strange circumstances, and at least in part, could one actually see it as good?

We pass by a section of the Sea of Galilee, briefly visible from the road. Robert remarks that vacationers are now waterskiing where Jesus walked. An impious image crosses my mind, of Jesus on water skis. I recall suddenly that this is the land of Jesus as well as of Abraham, this Jewish state where to the south and east of us Jerusalem teems with the holiest places in Christendom. Why is it disconcerting to picture Jesus going about his work in the land of the Jews? Perhaps because that is the way the later Christians wanted it; to convey the idea that while Jesus was himself a Jew, he was also a vastly superior Jew, one in whom the entire revision of an unworthy people was latent and foretold. In terms of an old joke, it was funny, Jesus did not look Jewish, nor did he behave Jewish either, not as behaving Jewish came to be caricatured and condemned in Europe and the New World. No moneylender he, no conniving materialist, no harsh, unbending disciplinarian either. This then was the Jew to end all Jews, an embodiment of salvation and self-destruction in a single, transitional figure.

The recollection of his presence here had some bearing on my inquiry—if not directly on the children, then on the nation that shapes them. If the image of Jesus in Israel seems odd in the modern imagination, did it also seem out of place when Jesus was alive? Beneath the newly planted plums and avocados, one pictures the ancient deserts as they were: the fierce sun cracking down on the driest yellow; the remorseless distances; the lines of horizon stretched taut like piano wires across everything that was still, flat and empty. The sky was white or it was black. One burned in the morning and froze at night. Who could survive in such a region but those who became like the region itself, tough to the point of brutality, with edges exposed everywhere.

That is the way one sees the God of the Old Testament as well, a figure like a titanic sword, full of beautiful and dangerous angles. He called himself a jealous God, and He behaved like one, conjuring tests of piety and loyalty so severe as to suggest near madness in His passion with His own power. One only has to read Exodus to realize the capacity of this God; how He deliberately hardened and rehardened the heart of Pharaoh, hardened it against the acquiescence Pharaoh was prepared to give, thus always making it necessary to deliver yet one more plague. No rationalist He, the God of the Old Testament did not want the Egyptian to be persuaded by conscience or practicality to let the children of Israel go. What God wanted clearly was to prove His own extreme might, mysterious, benumbing; to prove it to Pharaoh, to the Jews, perhaps to Himself. He was a perfect God for a desert.

And then, nearly two thousand years after Abraham, this younger God comes along, so unlike his father in temperament. Oh, he was a Middle Easterner, all right. He could shout at the apostles and make a ruckus in the temples, and he could even, in the Sermon on the Mount, sound occasionally menacing as he laid down the new law. But the message he bore was so different from his father's, so much more patient and rational, quite absent of hard edges. Were the ancient Jews, then, grown tired of the old harshness and rage? Were they ready, some of them, for a God who would let them go a bit easier on themselves, or who might at least be more explicit about his standards? The thought seems apt in modern Israel, where the latest Jews may also be tiring of the hardness that is necessary to preserve a threatened nation.

Yet the thought also seems presumptuous, out of line. I remind myself where I am—in a country of real people, with a real history. If ever a nation had a right to hardness, it is this one. Israel itself is a child of war. Born in one war, fighting another at the age of eight, another at nineteen, yet another at twenty-one, and the wars continue. Its founders are children of war as well. As Robert reminded me, many of the parents of the children at Manara were among those who survived the concentration camps, who as children of war themselves watched babies hurled into white-hot ovens and small boys hung on the gallows. My own Berliner relatives whose names I do not even know lie in ashes among the dead children of war—if the black hell Hitler gave the world is to be called merely a war. No one who did not experience that hell can ever know what it means to live after it. Not I, certainly, who played capture the flag in Gramercy Park while my cousins were lined up at Birkenau.

I watch Eddie study the countryside from his self-cornered position in the backseat. Throughout our visit, I noticed how dramatically edgy Eddie seemed much of the time. He attributed his edginess to not getting the sort of pictures he wanted, but I think it had more to do with his feeling out of place. He never said so to me, perhaps because he thought that, being Jewish, I would feel quite at home in Israel. I probably looked less ill at ease than Eddie because I was more familiar

75

with the ways Jews deal with each other. Social tricks like seizing the offensive in an argument or suddenly touching one's opponent in order to indicate: (a) that you love him, and (b) that you would have struck him otherwise, were not strange to me, and so I may have appeared comfortable among my own people. But I was no more a reborn Israeli than was Eddie, and in several ways I was less so.

For one thing, Israel does little actively to make a stranger feel immediately welcome. I think this too has something to do with the fact of the country's youth, that wittingly or not, Israelis often behave like a club of children whenever a new kid approaches. So much is yet to be determined and codified within the club by its own members—purposes, directions, leaders—that the presence of a stranger automatically serves as a disruption. If he is just passing through, it is hardly worth the effort of the group as a whole to make an adjustment to him. If he is here for the duration, then (asked warily) what sort of adjustments will his presence require? For Eddie and me, the passers-through, no adjustments were advisable, and none were made. I did not mind this in the least, and I would be surprised if, deep down, Eddie did either. Every reporter knows the self-contempt that comes from passing oneself off as a member of the family of the people he interviews, and then, in the cold quiet of the room with the typewriter, having to turn against that former family in the interests of a perceived truth. Israelis preempt such mortification.

My own particular reason for feeling like an outsider in Israel was simply that my father would never have gone there, and I, his oldest son, was feeling his attitude in me. I realized, after no more than two days in the country, that I had not been afraid to return to Israel, as I initially thought, because it might presage a new disaster like my father's death, but because he, alive in me, was withholding my heart from the place. When I considered it, my first abortive visit to Israel might have been conceived as an intentional affront to my father, the way I used to poke around the Lower East Side as a child and deliberately make him nervous by my interest in the world he had associated with poverty and ignorance and thus had cast away, en route to becoming a distinguished physician, a respectable American. I had no such world to cast away. Yet I was feeling something of the discomfort with my own people that my father felt. And I was ashamed of this feeling.

Still, the feeling was both mine and his. I suppose that my experiencing it was a simple example of the child taking on the characteristics of the parent. But these adoptions may be more deliberate, more earnestly willed than one realizes. To be, in any way, one's mother or father is itself an act of reconciliation, a sign that one is prepared to make an extreme gesture of peace by wholly sympathizing with one's antagonist. Such a gesture is a show of homage, of filial piety exactly as Confucius prescribed it: "Of all creatures produced by Heaven and Earth, man is the noblest. Of all man's actions there is none greater than filial piety." The connection is clear. Life is noble; parents give children life; parents are noble. One must pay the debt of one's life to the people who made that life, a reason perhaps that a tenet of Confucianism is that children should never leave their parents during their lifetime. The adoption of one's parents' thoughts is a way of never leaving them, and when they finally leave you, you have by then taken so much of them in that the giving of life has been reciprocated.

So abstract a revelation held no particular consolation for me, but it did add a consideration to the journey. Up to this point on the trip I had been thinking of a tendency toward war making as something that was taught to children either by indoctrination, by experience, or both. Yet the few children I met so far who had suffered a good deal of indoctrination and too much experience appeared, for the most part, unscathed. What, then, of some of the other, more universal, elements that go to develop a mind? What of the dead father whose fears and prejudices were so enmeshed with his valor and generosities that the strengthening elements could not be, or would not be, absorbed without the frailties going with them? At first I was thinking of myself, but then I was picturing Bernadette's stubborn face and seeing in it something that one day in the future she might not successfully suppress. The process of learning to love one's parents is so arduous, we could easily take on a parent's wars to achieve that love.

Such a thought delimits the idea that the urge to fight wars is a genetic inheritance of the species by narrowing it down to one's immediate family, but it makes the urge no more palatable. It may in fact be scarier to consider that war, rather than being born in you, is an impulse you give birth to yourself in order to come to terms with your forebears. This was merely a daydream speculation on my part, one whose origin may have been so personal as to make it inapplicable to the lives of the children I met so far, or was to meet. But it was worthwhile keeping in mind that the children of war suffer the internal wars of children everywhere, and of every time.

It was with this idea of parental inheritance that I approached Dr. Kalman Benyamini that evening in Jerusalem. Dr. Benyamini is a professor of psychology, specializing in children and youth, at the Hebrew University of Jerusalem, and the director of the Jerusalem Municipal Psychology Service. He trains people like Zion and Leah. His home is very dark, located in what appears to be an ancient neighborhood of the city. It has high-vaulted ceilings and an antique elegance, like some of the older apartments on the Upper West Side of New York; the sort of place where one suspects great conversations occur, but is not quite sure he would care to live there. Such homes are reminiscent of Central Europe. So is Dr. Benyamini. He is tall and wiry, looks about sixty, with a studious face but a kind one. All these psychologists, it seems, have kind, studious faces.

On the matter of inherited hate, he is plainly practical: "Young people will go along with adults in recognizing political facts." The fact is that Israel has enemies, so in this country the grown-up's enemies will be the child's as well. Indeed, society as a whole sometimes functions as the parent here, to adults

78

and to children alike. There is a strong personal identification with the country. When Dr. Benyamini worked as an army psychologist, he saw patients who would cry out, "I am the Jewish nation, and look what they did to me!" He recalls a carpenter, a tank driver in the Yom Kippur War, whose comrades were killed when their tank was hit. The carpenter's injuries were psychological. "I'm Golda," he shouted in the hospital. "And they caught me with my pants down. And they kicked me!"

"Is individuality in children discouraged, then?"

"Well, let's say that Israel is not a hothouse for breeding individuality. Our kids are much more group conforming than you find in other northern countries." (Like many other Israelis, he sees Israel as a northern country.) Here too he cites the Army, as an instrument of uniformity. "On the other hand," he adds, "army service has a very strong influence on consolidating one's values. It is not an empty duty here. It has to do with actual circumstances, and this has effects for better and worse. For worse, our kids have little chance to find themselves in a humanistic, self-searching way. At the same time, they don't have the normal egotism of youth either."

Asked if the continual atmosphere of war makes Israeli children more violent than others, he says: "To the contrary. Kids are much less violent here. They fight less. They are much less violent than adults. War is a necessity to them. It is not something that is in the conscience of every individual." He mentions his own childhood, when his family employed an Arab on their farm for many years. "Then suddenly one day he wasn't there anymore. He was the head of a gang that attacked one of our neighbors. But has that instilled in me a personal hatred of Arabs? Not necessarily. Not more than my straightforward allegiance to the society."

We discuss the fact that an allegiance to society at least in part means an allegiance to hatred, if not an individual hatred of Arabs, then of Arabs in the mass. He allows that the presence of a common enemy has made the society more homogenous and more cooperative in its reactions, yet it hasn't created a new Prussia or Sparta. "This is not a tidy culture. This is a Mediterranean culture. Human relations are not formalized here, as they are in Protestant countries. There is no smile number seventeen for a specific social contingency. The people are more candid, more pushy. They are also very generous." He cites the example of a recent campaign for Cambodian relief. "It was a *competition* for generosity."

What he wishes to emphasize is that in spite of the fact that Israel has grown up with war, and that wars have shaped its social institutions, its way of life, nonetheless Israelis are not a bellicose people. So far, he says, all of Israel's wars have been necessary. If the country should ever find itself engaged in an unnecessary war, he says, eight months before the invasion of Lebanon and the capture of Beirut, "We'll fight, we won't betray the country, but it won't be the same kind of history."

I mention that 30 per cent of the Israeli population is under fifteen years of age. What will the next generation be like? That too, he says, will depend on external circumstances. "I don't know what peace would do to us. The crisis in Israel at the moment is an adult crisis. The adult society does not know which way to go, and yet it has to show which way to go." He discusses the difficulties that children face in this regard and slides into a momentary reverie. Then suddenly he looks up and makes a remark connected to nothing. "But they are beautiful youngsters," he says.

On Sunday, September 27, the day before Rosh Hashana, we drive, Robert, Eddie and I, to visit two Israeli settlements on the West Bank: Kfar Etzion to the south of Jerusalem and Beit Hadassah in Hebron. Robert explains that Kfar Etzion was originally a Jewish settlement before 1948 but that it fell to the Jordanians who, during Israel's war for independence, opened fire on the settlement gratuitously. Children of the settlement were evacuated before the adults were slaughtered while making a last stand. Kfar Etzion, says Robert, is a kind of Israeli Alamo. It was reclaimed by some of the original surviving children in 1970 and is now a thriving kibbutz.

80

Beit Hadassah was started at Kiryat Arba', a neighborhood of apartment blocks in a suburb of Hebron. In 1929 Arabs massacred the Jews in Kiryat Arba' while the British looked on and did nothing to protect them. After the 1967 War a woman named Miriam Luddinger took her eleven children and marched back to reclaim the apartments in a much disputed land grab. Robert tells us that the settlement is under heavy guard these days and has been attacked by the PLO.

Heading south out of Jerusalem, we honk donkeys off the road and ride past Bethlehem. Robert points out the site of a Herodian palace. I remember Marianne Moore's poem about the mind being "an enchanted thing" and "not a Herod's oath that cannot change." Children on the brain. Children and the past. It occurs to me that I have been searching out the world's newcomers in the most ancient of places: children among the ruins, children playing where time has taken the ruins away. Yesterday, driving down from the north, we passed a monument by the roadside of a kid's bike on a pedestal of stone. Wreaths of leaves were done up as wheels. Shortly afterward, we could see the Jordan River, and then Jericho, where we stopped to take fruit juice from some soldiers at a roadblock. A little farther on we paused again at another patrol where Eddie shot pictures and I mesmerized an Arab boy with the old thumb trick, in which it appears that I am removing the top half of my thumb. A little farther still we passed part of the Zin Desert, where Moses wandered. Children and the past.

Now the sun fills everything with hot light as we pull up at Kfar Etzion and take in the quiet. The white walls of the houses are so bright I cannot look at them without squinting. Eddie searches for subjects. Robert starts a conversation with two young people who are passing by. They appear to be in their thirties. The man wears a bright plaid shirt, maroon shorts and a yarmulke. The woman, also in bright shirt and shorts, has an intense, though not cheerless face. Her name is Sima, his Jerry, and they have been close friends all their lives. They identify themselves as Child Number 46 and Child Number 50

81

respectively. These, they explain, are the designations they were given when as infants they were evacuated before their parents fought at the "Alamo."

Sima was nine months old when the war of 1948 began, Jerry three months. They and the other children of the settlement were taken first to the basement of a monastery in Jerusalem, until it could be determined how many adults of Kfar Etzion had survived. Jerry's father was killed in the last battle of Kfar Etzion. Sima's was wounded, but he recovered to take care of Jerry and Sima and many of the other children who were orphaned in the fighting. The children of Kfar Etzion stayed together, found cohesion in each other. Jerry recalls they were so clannish that when they went to school they dressed alike in the outfits of the settlement rather than in school uniforms.

When they grew up they did not lose touch with each other either. They had a saying as children: "Next year in Kfar Etzion." Every summer they convened in a camp where the original Kfar Etzion was physically recreated: "Yellow Hill, Rust Hill—we replicated the sites of Kfar Etzion to keep them alive in our minds."

"And when we went to pray in the cemetery," Jerry continues, "we always prayed together. Because our parents were killed in a massacre, there was a mass grave, a 'brothers grave,' we called it. After prayers we would go to the top of a hill and stand together and point to an oak tree in the distance which came to symbolize Kfar Etzion."

"I felt that I knew Jerry's father," says Sima, "from the pictures of him. I felt that I knew all the fathers who were killed. We were part of history class in school. The other children studied about Kfar Etzion. We always talked about returning." Twelve of the original number did so.

"Do you feel the presence of the fathers in this place now?"

"In everyday life, no," says Jerry. "In memorial services, yes, of course." Children and the past. We are shown around a museum in the settlement where the past is preserved in a cool modern room. These two were born as Israel was born. Now Jerry has three children of his own who he hopes will also make their lives at Kfar Etzion. This seems both beautiful and suffocating to me, but I hold my tongue.

At noon we stop at Beit Hadassah. This is the last Israeli settlement I will see, the last Israeli place I will see for the present, as tomorrow, on Rosh Hashana, I will begin my visits with the Palestinians. There is hardly any activity in Beit Hadassah at this hour. Eddie rounds up some children in the playground, trying to get a picture of them and of the Israeli guards standing over them on a wall. The guard holds a Galil assault rifle. A belligerent construction worker with a stubble beard and a stupid face starts up with Eddie for the hell of it. He carries an Uzi machine gun. Photographers, I begin to notice, are always given a much harder time than reporters; something about the absolute truth of pictures, I imagine, or the blatant intrusion. Eddie turns to Robert for help, who diplomatically tells the construction worker to move on. The worker then approaches me and announces angrily that he fought in Korea.

I look down at the playground. It consists of small spring rides, like hobby horses, with the faces of Mickey Mouse and Pluto where the horses' heads should be. The slide has Donald Duck's head in a blue sailor's cap mounted at the top of the steps. When the children climb up they enter Donald's head from the rear and slide down his tongue, painted red. The children are too fascinated with Eddie and his cameras to pose naturally, and Robert implores them to play as they would were we not here. I cross Shallela Street in order to remove yet one more distraction from the scene, and comb the dust-filled empty lot where once three Arab stores stood side by side.

These three stores were demolished by the Israeli Army after an incident in May 1980. Terrorists climbed atop the roofs of the stores one Friday evening, waiting for the residents of Beit Hadassah to return from evening prayers at the Tomb of the Patriarch, just up the road. The tomb is where Abraham and Isaac are said to lie buried. At 7:40 P.M., as the people from

83

Beit Hadassah were about to re-enter their apartment building, the terrorists fired on them, wounding sixteen and killing six. The store owners had willingly allowed the terrorists to use their roofs, and for that their establishments were destroyed. Now, where the stores were, a small hill rises to a white-gray wall bearing hieroglyphic scars. Olive trees, stunted, with gaps in their trunks, appear about to topple.

The pedestrian traffic picks up a bit as I look on sleepily. An Arab woman walks by with a huge beige urn balanced on her head like a stubby cannon. Little children, returning from outings, tag far behind their parents and disappear suddenly behind a fleet of smoking, noisy trucks. A father walks hand in hand with his son. A small boy slogs along holding a briefcase half his size, trying to keep up with a bigger girl, his sister, it seems, who has great oversized pants cuffs rolled almost to her knees. A baby, still a crawler, sits in a doorway, her legs stuck out in a V, and gapes, amazed, at everyone who leaves and enters the building. I scan the building's wall and stop at a window high up which overlooks both the place where the three stores were and the Beit Hadassah playground.

There an Arab boy sits, half-hidden behind a faded pink curtain, peering out from a barred window that resembles a birdcage and staring at the Israeli children shouting in the playground. He dangles his legs through the bars and does not move. I watch him watch the others, wondering what he sees. I assume that his view extends beyond Beit Hadassah to the Tomb of the Patriarch, of Abraham, the father of both the Arabs and the Jews, who was ready to sacrifice his son for the God he worshiped.

FOUR

·⊶·

Palestinians

According to the doctor on the case, who lacked a standard medical term to describe it, the child was born in a "cesarean section by explosion." The delivery occurred in July 1981 during an Israeli air raid of the Fakhani area of West Beirut, a neighborhood where PLO offices were located. The child's mother, nine months pregnant, ran in panic from her apartment house in an effort to elude the falling bombs. There were no witnesses to what exactly happened next, but when the shelling stopped, Mrs. Halaby was found dead in the rubble with her stomach ripped open. Three meters away, still enveloped in the placenta, lay her new baby girl. She was given the name "Palestine."

This story was told me the first evening of my arrival in Beirut, where Palestine's birth was already famous and emerging into modern Palestinian folklore. In fact, the baby was named Palestine not by her father, but by committee, since the circumstances of her birth were as politically useful as they were miraculous. The child would be the state of Palestine itself: born out of destruction, indomitable, pure of heart. By the time I learned of her existence, her eye-tight baby's face had been photographed repeatedly in local newspapers and magazines and sent abroad on postcards and pamphlets pleading the Palestinian cause and seeking donations. She was the inspiration for songs and poems. No one could mention the subject of children in Beirut without invoking the legend of the baby Palestine.

Yet that night over dinner at the Hotel Commodore, the subjects of Palestine and of children in general come second to the main event of the day. Eddie and I are sitting with Mahmoud Labadi, the head of PLO press relations in West Beirut, in the Commodore's justifiably notorious Chinese restaurant. Labadi is a quiet man of forty-one who keeps his own counsel and wears an ambiguous expression. The meeting was arranged by Abu Said, thirty-one years a correspondent for *Time,* admired widely in the Middle East for various qualities, including discretion, fair play and horse sense. The hotel employees treat him like the owner, as in fact does the owner. Kings know him. In his forties he is said to have been Clark Gablish handsome. Even now, in his seventies, a kind of reverent gossip promotes him as a ladies' man, as much a tribute to Abu Said's stature as to the imagination. He set up this dinner so that Eddie and I could obtain passes from Labadi to visit Palestinian camps and other institutions. The PLO would thus control what we saw in Lebanon, but I doubted they would be able to control my questions or the children's answers. I soon learned it was unnecessary for them to do so.

At the moment, the subject is the car bomb. That morning at nine-thirty, Wafik Al Tibi Street was almost obliterated by a bomb planted in a parked car filled with one hundred kilos of TNT and eighty liters of gasoline. The PLO press office is located on Wafik Al Tibi Street, along with several eight- to ten-story modern white apartment houses, typical of West Beirut, packed side by side. Eighty-three people were killed and 225 wounded. Labadi himself only avoided the explosion by uncharacteristically arriving late to work. Everyone who stops by our table to commiserate with him offers an opinion on who did the bombing. The suspects are regulars: the Syrians, the Israelis, the Phalangists or any combination of these. So far, the one group to take "credit" for the act is a new one called the Front for the Liberation of Lebanon from Foreigners.

In retrospect, I realize that this bombing was an apt introduction to Lebanon, though now, after having seen Beirut the following summer, a single street explosion seems relatively tame. At the time, in late September, the incident was unusually severe and unnerving. Yet it was hardly shocking to a city that for seven years had known unrelenting violence. Some sixty thousand lives were lost during Lebanon's civil war of 1975–76, roughly the number of casualties the U.S. suffered in fourteen years in Viet Nam. Until the summer of 1982, destruction since the civil war had been limited to Israeli reprisals against the PLO, sporadic battles of the Syrians, Phalangists and Palestinians, and the ordinary run of assassinations and street bombings such as the one occurring that morning.

The odd thing to observe, however, is the general Lebanese resilience in the face of such things. Either the Lebanese are the most durable people in the world, or they have achieved a nirvana of terror that has equipped them with an unearthly jauntiness in the presence of disaster. The country was to display its resilience to the world that following summer, and it was showing that same spirit now. At the time of my first visit the sight of a new bank going up in Beirut was as common as a bashed-in Mercedes. You could not tell if a hole in the ground was the work of a rocket or of a construction team. Shops flourished (as they did during the worst of the bombing in July). There must be something about the Lebanese eagerness to do business, to keep businesses going, an inheritance from the Phoenician traders perhaps, that simply will not permit them to capitulate to ruin. On my second visit I would find this quality less admirable than appalling, but either way it was astonishing to witness.

My purpose in going there this first time, however, was not to talk with the Lebanese children—that would come in July—but to continue meeting with the Palestinians. This I had started to do on the West Bank after visiting the Israeli settlements there. The day following my brief stops at Kfar Etzion and Beit Hadassah in Hebron, I began talking with Palestinian children in El Bireh and Ramallah, about fifteen miles north of Jerusalem, and now I sought to extend my inquiry into Lebanon. It was instructive meeting the same people in two wholly different countries, a quick way to grasp what Palestinians mean when they describe themselves as a people without a nation. For such a people an event like the baby Palestine's birth becomes a major symbol of cohesion.

Eddie and I ask Labadi if we can see the child. Labadi will try to locate her. Meanwhile, he will provide us with guides and translators. For his part, Abu Said gives us Saleem, a bull-necked Druze, reputed to be the best driver in Beirut. This is no slight honor in a city where the high road is the sidewalk, and the favorite gear *reverse*. Saleem soon proves that his fame rests as much on his serene temperament as on his skill.

Still, Saleem cannot deliver us to the door of the PLO press office on Wafik Al Tibi Street the following morning. Because of yesterday's car bombing we are stopped every fifty feet in the area and made to show our identifications. The car trunk is opened and reopened. Eventually I come to recognize the slamming of a car trunk as one of Beirut's indigenous sounds. Saleem gets us as close as possible to the end of the street. The air is gray and acrid with clouds of disinfectant shot from pipes mounted like cannons on the backs of pickup trucks. This spraying is done, explains Eddie, who saw the same thing in Viet Nam, because of the dead bodies and the danger of disease. Children linger in the doorways to watch a bulldozer push away fragments of wood and broken bricks. The devastation is enormous. Windows seven stories up are jagged holes. Huge slabs of debris are thrown down from the damaged buildings, glass hitting the pavement with the noise of brief, sudden applause. A strange-looking boy in a clay-orange T-shirt skips along the sidewalk, deliberately dancing out in front of the falling glass. His mind is lost in some private game. His eyes roll back, showing only whites.

Asam, our guide, will take us to the Institute of Tel Zaatar, called variously Defiance Home and Steadfastness Home. Asam, a good party man, prefers that we call it Steadfastness Home; he thinks the name more virtuous. The institute was founded to provide shelter, foster parents and education for 313 Palestinian children whose parents were killed in the Tel Zaatar massacre of 1976. A year before that massacre twenty-seven Palestinian residents of the Tel Zaatar refugee camp were gunned down by Christian Phalangists as they were returning home by bus from a political rally. The rally was to celebrate a terrorist attack on Qiryat Shemona. (I begin to take these connections for granted in the war zones.) In 1976 there was a full-scale attack on the camp itself in which the Phalangists used 75-mm. and 155-mm. howitzers during a seven-week siege. Three thousand people died, and Tel Zaatar was destroyed.

The orphanage is a large vanilla-colored house with a facade of balconies and a graceful courtyard out front. There are 160 children living here now, not all of them victims of Tel Zaatar. A small boy whose mother was killed while bringing him water from a well refused to take water from anyone when he first arrived at the home, fearing that water augured death. This is told us by the tall, sad-eyed man who runs the home. Soon, he says proudly, the boy recovered. Another boy of two, who was carried in his father's arms when the man was shot to death, made no sound whatever during his first six months in the home. Now, says the tall man, that child is prattling normally.

Jamila, Boutros and Mona have been at the Institute of Tel Zaatar since it opened. Now sixteen, sixteen and seventeen respectively, they are considered elders among the children and have assumed the responsibilities of parents to the younger ones. They sit in a row on a bed in one of the "family rooms," mostly beds and dressers. The room is sun-filled and feels warm despite the linoleum on the floor and the limited furnishings. Jamila, though in sneakers and pigtails, looks older than the other two because of the depth of her eyes and the prominence of her cheekbones. Her parents were killed when she was ten, during an Israeli shelling of Tyre, in the refugee camp of Rashidieh. Boutros's father, killed when the boy was eight, was shot to death when the Phalangists raided his poultry farm. "He was hit beside the heart." The boy's voice shakes slightly as he indicates the wound's location on his own chest.

Mona lost her father in Tel Zaatar itself. The girl has short dark hair and a baby face that looks alternately cheerful and scared:

"When Tel Zaatar was under attack by the Phalangists, my family was living with my grandparents. During the attack the roads were closed and we remained in hiding, but when the camp fell we tried to escape. Buildings on both sides of the roads were burned and damaged. We took shelter in them. I was ten at the time. My family divided into two groups, my mother going with my grandparents, I with my father, brothers and sisters. In the night the Phalangists came upon us, and they began to shoot. I fainted. They must have thought they killed me. When I awoke in the middle of the night, all of them, my father, my brothers, my sisters, were dead, lying around me in the room."

Several small children stomp by, shouting in the hallway. Boutros claps his hands twice rapidly to silence them. They quiet down immediately.

Jamila observes that by losing their parents they have lost their childhood as well. "We are not normal children," she says, detached. Like the girls in Belfast, these three have been forced to grow up quickly. "I have spent now five years at this home," says Boutros, "and I feel like a man." His mustache almost makes him look like a man.

Asked if they believe they have gained anything worthwhile from their tragedies, Boutros replies, "Power." His face seems amiable for the answer. What he means by power is something specific: "To regain our homeland." At that, all three talk at once.

"First we were driven from Palestine in 1948."

"The Israelis tried to exterminate us."

"It's not their land, it's our land!" says Jamila. Her voice is urgent. As the others continue in this vein for a few minutes, Jamila notices that I am sitting in an uncomfortable position on the bed opposite them. Without a word she rises and slips a pillow behind the small of my back.

Whom do they most admire in the world? "Our great chairman Arafat," says Boutros. Asam is visibly pleased to make the translation, and he gives it dramatic emphasis. I am reminded that his mission here is public relations. "After Arafat, there are Ho Chi Minh and Castro," says Boutros. For Jamila it is Lenin: "Because he made a new world for his people. He made them care for themselves and work together."

"Is it more important to work with others or to be an individual?"

"To work with others," she says. "But everyone must make something of himself first. To study, to learn, to be *someone*. After that he can cooperate with society." The others nod in approval. Is knowledge a kind of strength? Boutros takes the question back to politics: "We lost Palestine. Israel occupied Palestine. All we do is talk." I ask why he thinks people make war. "First we were driven from Palestine. The Israelis tried to exterminate us . . ."

"But why *generally* do people make war?"

Jamila: "We don't want war. We're *obliged* to make war." I make certain that Asam is translating the abstract nature of my questions accurately. He assures me he is.

They are asked what books they like to read. For Mona it is detective stories. "And Tolstoy, *Anna Karenina*." No, she smiles, there is no Count Vronsky in her life. Boutros reads about the subject of war. He is finishing Clausewitz at the moment. Jamila admires Gorki, and has just read *Oliver Twist*.

91

Does *Oliver Twist* remind her of life in the orphanage? "There is no connection," she says. "He lived in the streets with strangers, but I am living in a home."

The question of their future is raised, and once again the three of them direct the topic to Palestine's future glory. Jamila adds something more: "If I could shape the future of the whole world, I would forbid the use of all sophisticated weapons—neutron bombs and things like them—even if it is in the interests of my people. Otherwise we will destroy ourselves."

"Do you all plan to marry and have children of your own?"

"Yes," says Jamila playfully. "But not right now." They laugh. Mona blushes. Boutros jumps in: "When I was very young my parents told me about leaving Palestine. I depended on them for everything. For me it will be different. I will teach my children to depend on themselves, as I now depend on myself." Will he teach love to his children? Will he tell them to love all peoples? "Yes," he says definitely. "I will teach them to love all people who love the Palestinians."

Before leaving the building, Asam guides us to a classroom where a deeply tanned fat man plays an instrument called an oud, which looks like a lute, and leads a chorus of small children. The children sit at their desks facing the front of the room and sing absentmindedly, clearly knowing the song so well they do not require adult direction. The verses are sung quietly, but the refrain, "Pal-es-teen!" shakes the room. I heard a song much like it in a Palestinian school on the West Bank a few days earlier. The children were fundamentally the same in both places: singing about Palestine, reciting poems about Palestine, speaking of Palestine with anger, hope, resolve and unanimity.

The essential difference lay in the spirit of the children, there being far more obvious melancholy and bitterness on the West Bank. In Ramallah a stunningly beautiful sixteen-year-old girl named Waffa, dressed royally in a long-sleeved off-white blouse, said calmly that whenever she looks at an Israeli, any Israeli, she sees not a person but "an enemy, only an enemy."

Her father has twice been hauled off to jail by the Israeli authorities, and he was in jail as Waffa and I spoke. Asked if she felt pity when she heard of an attack on Israelis in which children are killed, Waffa answered: "It is a matter of mathematics. The more Israelis who die, the more Arabs there will be. Therefore," explained the beautiful girl, "eventually we will be in control."

Other West Bank children were not as harsh, but were no less embittered. A senior boy in a Quaker school in Ramallah, a lanky tennis player named Nabil, said that he does not think of Jews as his enemies, only Zionists. While condemning Israeli parents for preaching hate to their children, he conceded that Palestinian parents often do the same by urging revenge. Hania, a fifteen-year-old in the same Quaker school, who was shot in the leg during a student demonstration, foreswore revenge. Even if she had had a gun at the moment the Israeli soldier fired on her, she said, she could not have shot back. Yet when I asked Hania the question I put to the three in Beirut, about what they would teach their own children, the girl looked away. "I would not bring children into this world," she said.

Of course, the difference in the children's spirit in Lebanon and on the West Bank was based on the difference of circumstance. Children on the West Bank live under Israel's thumb. Nabil, who has been beaten up by Israeli soldiers for loitering on a street after a school dance, said that he felt his life had been robbed of essential freedoms. Asked how he knew that, when he had never experienced such freedoms, he answered, "You feel it inside you." In contrast, the Palestinian children in Lebanon think and do much as they please. Since the Palestinians emigrated to Lebanon after King Hussein expelled them from Jordan in September 1970, and since they subsequently—and violently—took over most of the country, their children were not only free, but openly urged, to express their nationalistic pride and aspirations.

Political conditions aside, however, the children of both the West Bank and Lebanon were clearly of a single, unified people. Geography and individual circumstances seemed to affect neither their zeal nor singlemindedness. I expected to find the latter more irritating and disconcerting than in fact I did. By the time I met the three children in the Tel Zaatar orphanage, two things were evident about the children's sense of nationalism, beside its patent sincerity. One was that it was not solely the product of their elders' indoctrination; both their fervor and the antipathies of these children arose from tragedies and humiliations they had experienced firsthand. The other, oddly, was that this ardent, monotonous nationalism was apparently not harmful to the children. In its way it offered them a purpose for living, where much else in their lives had tried to take all purposes away.

Still, listening to children like Boutros, Nabil and the others, one wonders how they can work up such enthusiasm for a place they never saw and a life they never led. To the Palestinian children here in Lebanon, or on the West Bank, or anywhere, the idea of original Palestine must have all the trappings of Utopia. Children favor dreamlands readily. Therefore the image of Palestine as a place where all wrongs will be righted, all problems solved, all lives made fruitful, must have a propaganda value of its own, quite independent of the nostalgia or resentment which their parents, or more likely their grandparents, inevitably bring to the subject. To a large extent, the Palestinian children probably do not need their elders to keep the faith alive in them. Behold Palestine, a genuine Oz. It may be reclaimed not by magic or a spiritual pilgrimage, but by guns, something tangible. For Palestinian adults the element of fantasy is at once heightened and diminished, since one may both describe and recollect Palestine as a land of unearthly contentment and point to it as something real, lying on the other side of the hills. For children the fantasy never diminishes, and is almost too good to be true. Not only are they allowed to live a folktale; they are blessed by adults as they do so. Instead of being required, like children elsewhere, to learn to distinguish between dreams and realities, these kids are encouraged to fuse them.

On the road south the following morning, Eddie and I ask Amer, our guide for this particular excursion, if we are likely to see child guerrillas training with weapons. Eddie is especially eager for this, because there are so few photographs that can illustrate at a glance the subject of children and war, and the sight of a small boy or girl carrying an M1 is memorable. But Amer is wary of our interest, feeling that the children will be represented solely as warriors. The PLO wishes to have it both ways. Eventually, we persuade him that military training is but one aspect of a Palestinian child's life with which we are concerned, and he agrees to let us see "a little." In order to see anything at all, however, one must first stop at the office of Colonel Azmi in Tyre, a visit that I considered a waste of time when I learned that it was necessary but which eventually (that following summer) became connected to the heart of the entire journey.

For the moment, I sit back in the car and survey the Mediterranean on our right: flat, blue and boatless. We pass a stationary Ferris wheel near the beach, which I had glimpsed on several drives around Beirut and had come to regard as an emblem of the nation's death as an amusement center. We drive through the last checkpoint, one manned by Syrians, then down past signs advertising "Kangaroo Beach" and "Family Beach—Five Stars," play areas where thousands of impoverished Arabs now live as squatters. Near the Haroun Al-Rachid restaurant, men fly-cast from boulders stuck out in the water. The day is hot and white, as ever. Amer points out the rusted, unused railroad tracks running beside the sea, where a boy in a work shirt strolls with a rifle on his shoulder. Eddie and I saw the same tracks in the north of Israel.

Saleem steers the car carefully through the narrow streets of Damur, a town besieged by Palestinians and Moslems in 1976, where thousands of Christian Lebanese were either murdered or driven from their homes. Ahead, we can see Sidon, a pile of misty chalk in the middle distance. This is midmorning Sunday, but Sidon is already busy with traffic and the trilling of car horns. Through a gap in an ancient wall, I catch sight of the Castle of St. Louis, the red and ocher "sea castle," whose walls are reinforced by sawed-off columns that stick out between the rectangular stones like heads without faces. When the Crusaders built that castle Sidon was already part of the old world. In the *Iliad* Achilles offers the prize of a silver mixing bowl that was crafted in Sidon. In the *Odyssey* a woman from Sidon seduces one of Odysseus' men. Little is seductive here now, the town seeming to consist merely of ruins upon ruins. "The journalists are our only tourists," says Amer, who talks less guardedly than Asam. Upon my asking him, he explains that his gnarled right hand is the result of a bomb blast.

"To the south we will see banana farms," he tells us. So we do, along with the remains of an oil refinery bombed by the Israelis. At a roadside stand, toys are for sale beside a gas station called "Phoenicia." Burned-out cars lie heaped on the shoulders of the highway like cattle skulls. There was much shelling in this region even before the summer of 1982. Amer points to where the PLO are rebuilding a bridge connecting the city of Tyre to the rest of south Lebanon. We are in Tyre now. Tyre, from which the court architect of King Hiram was dispatched to build the Temple of Solomon. Tyre, mentioned by Ezekiel, visited by Zeus. Like Sidon, it too is forlorn, a mess. In the remnants of a Roman temple to Jupiter, Corinthian columns stand at great distances from each other like a minority of voters. A half-sunk ship sticks its nose out of the harbor.

We turn into a quiet neighborhood, pulling up at a grass hut mounted on top of a bunker in another bombed-out area. Here stands the PLO command post, the center of all military operations in southern Lebanon. The hut is furnished with red fake-leather office chairs set up in rows against the two long walls, at the far end of which is a large Swedish-modern desk. Behind the desk sits Colonel Azmi, chain-smoking Winstons.

He is blustery, impatient, a handsome man in his early

forties. Yes, yes, he will give us the passes we require, but first he has some words for the American people, which he would like Eddie and me to convey. Around the hut fifteen of his soldiers sit along the walls, as if at a town meeting. "We are ready!" shouts the colonel. Amer's muted translations work a nice counterpoint to the harangue. "We will not stop our struggle! We are not fascists! Our power is our arms! Kissinger brought on this trouble! We are not communists! Begin is a nazi!" I mention the purpose of our visit. "Children!" he shouts again. "We never intend to kill children." Then back to the theme. "To the last child we will struggle to regain our homeland!"

"Do you have children of your own, Colonel?" I ask him.

"I have one right here," he says, looking up as his son Samer enters the hut. Samer is four years old, about three and a half feet high, and dressed in matching black and white checkered shirt and pants, and polished black laced shoes. He strides regimentally toward the Swedish-modern desk and stands before his father.

"They are so young," explains the colonel. "But they are so proud." Then briskly to Samer: "Who is Sadat?"

"Sadat sold Palestine to Israel," says the boy, rapid-fire.

"Who is Jimmy Carter?"

"Carter supported Israel."

"Who are *you?*" asks his father with mock severity.

"I am from Palestine—from Hebron!"

"What is Israel?"

"The real name for Israel is Palestine."

The colonel invites me to ask questions of his son.

"Samer, have you thought of what you would like to do when you grow up?"

"I want to marry," says the boy. At that, the colonel's men, who have been sitting still and solemnly, explode with laughter. The boy blushes with shame and confusion. His father consoles him with a gesture of the hand. Asked if he would like to live in a world without soldiers, Samer says, "Yes," quietly. "I would love that." At his father's signal the boy exits.

"Colonel, would you send Samer into war?"

"I don't want him to suffer. But he would give his blood to regain his homeland. If I am killed, my son will carry my gun."

Months later, I learned that Colonel Azmi was reputed to have trained those who engineered many of the terrorist attacks on the north of Israel, including, most infamously, the coastal road massacre. Thus either his "We never intend to kill children" was an open lie, or the absence of intention was beside the point. I assumed he would attempt to justify such things to Samer in the name of the greater good, when he deemed Samer practical enough to place politics before people, or perhaps when Samer would be old enough to forgive him. As the events of the following summer proved, however, Colonel Azmi did not have much time left with Samer. And I, who believed I had seen the last of Colonel Azmi and his son that day in Tyre, would, in a sense, end my journey standing between the two of them.

At the refugee camp of Rashidieh Eddie takes pictures of children carrying guns while I wander among the shacks, kicking up dust as I go. This is where Jamila's parents were killed. I am told that nine thousand people live here now, but the camp seems almost totally deserted. A woman explains that two of the camp residents are getting married today and that many people are off at the wedding. By now the whiteness of the day is overwhelming: white roads, white walls, white sky at this hour. The old men of Rashidieh sip tea and soda at outdoor tables. On a wall a child has drawn an airplane with the Star of David on its fuselage, the plane bearing down on a boy riding a bicycle who does not see it coming. As I study it a skinny boy approaches with mischief all over his face.

"Hi, mister. *Parlez-vous français?*"

"*Un peu.*" I smile nervously and begin to fumble for French. "Vous *parlez français?*" I ask brightly.

"No," he giggles, sashaying away. "I speak English."

On a large hard-dirt field children are going through military exercises for Eddie's benefit. They hold their rifles chest high

98

and leap over bonfires, shouting savagely while twisting their bodies away from the flames. Afterward, Eddie has me pose with them, sitting on the ground in their midst like a counselor in a summer camp. The boys sing a patriotic song with roaring gusto. I pretend to be rattled by the noise and laugh with a pained expression, as if I am pleading for help. A boy touches my shoulder in a gesture of comradery. He laughs with my laughter. Then they all do, until the song is overcome with laughter, and the only sound remaining is laughter.

On the way back to Beirut, I consider again the question raised by Dror and Nimrod in Israel: Could a state of war do anything good for children? The answer in the long run was no, but it was not a no easily arrived at. Without a state of war, the small trainees of Rashidieh would seem to have no mission whatever in life. They would meander about in the poverty of their people until eventually they, like the elders of the refugee camp, would spend their days with their backs to the walls of their broken houses sucking on hookahs, foraging for memories and muttering to the young. As it is, thanks to present circumstances, they not only have a mission in life, but uniforms (albeit ragtag) and weapons to go with it. They have order and hierarchy. They are in fine physical condition. They have a sense of importance, of being essential both to a particular goal and an abstract idea. A state of war has provided all this.

But what good does such a state do for their insides, their well-being and character? The day after visiting Rashidieh I would meet a fifteen-year-old *ashbal,* a young guerrilla trainee, in Beirut, at once so fierce in his devotion to the PLO and so personally admirable that I could not imagine his virtues separated from conditions of violence, or nurtured anywhere else. "Let me have war," says one of the servants in *Coriolanus.* "It exceeds peace as far as the day does night," observing that peace makes people hate each other. To which another servant adds, "Reason, because they less need one another." Certainly, the Palestinian children feel needed, both spiritually and practically. If Jamila, Mona and Boutros are typical, they also readily respond to the needs of others. If asked, these children might well say that a state of war has made them more generous people, more sympathetic to the plights of their fellows, more aware of their responsibilities in the world.

Grown-ups make the same claims about war, and the claims are often proved. John Ruskin, of all people, once delivered a lecture to a British military academy in which he not only said that great art is impossible in a peaceful and peace-seeking country (Graham Greene had a similar thought when his Harry Lime of *The Third Man* credited the total progress of Swiss civilization with having arrived at the invention of the cuckoo clock), but also that the "full personal power of the human creature" is only achievable in war. An extreme position but not beyond the pale. A state of war offers every conceivable test of human values: courage, stamina, stoicism, intelligence, chivalry, cunning, loyalty, honor, self-sacrifice, coolheadedness, will. It also sharpens the senses, not simply because of the looming presence of danger, but because the existence of a common cause makes skillful discriminations necessary. War forces moral choices as well: the well-being of the group versus the pleasure or safety of the individual. And it sets up an embodiment of evil in the personage of the enemy, which in turn establishes a standard of moral good.

Friendship is also enhanced by a state of war, not comradeship alone, but genuine friendship born of deep affection and respect. One sees this in men at arms, of course, but also in those who are involved in a war but removed from the fighting —in journalists, for instance, who serve long tours in war zones. Foreign correspondents and war photographers like Eddie and Bill Pierce in Northern Ireland often grow very close to one another, and not simply because they have shared scary situations. The situations themselves have made them feel better about their work, more interesting as people, more alert, alive, in every sense improved. Elevated in such ways, they are worthy of strong friendships, and so their friendships are often formed on the highest grounds.

Then, too, the institution of an army provides stability for its members, a sort of roving state, equipped with its own laws and government. Children, who are natural conservatives, will make a family of such an institution; this is their territory, their place in the order of things. For the PLO children such grounding may be especially useful, since the Palestinians are in search of a place in the world themselves, and since they are fighting a guerrilla war, which means, as Franz Fanon said, that your country is where your toes are. Armies like the PLO and the IRA may hold a particular appeal for children, because they are both wild and conservative simultaneously, thus allowing more excitement within their stability than do the standing armed forces of an established power. They also enforce ideologies, as standing armies rarely do. A kid fighting with a bunch of rebels is far more apt to know why he is doing it than a recruit of a national guard.

Beside all this there is even a psychoanalytic theory which holds that a state of war may be beneficial for the subconscious in that it relieves it of self-contempt. All those teeming, implosive hatreds that make one an enemy of oneself are, in a state of war, deflected, discharged against a real enemy, who serves as guilt objectified. If there is any truth to such a theory, one would assume it applies to children as well as adults, even if children generally have fewer repressed impulses. Still, most children are afraid of some mystery or other—the wind, the dark, lightning and thunder—which may be dramatized forms of their anxieties. Should these anxieties be transformed into the recognizable and familiar figure of a man, then the enemy, whoever he is, ought to become considerably less terrifying, perhaps conquerable. War which is good for the body, the soul and the mind would also be good for the psyche.

Finally, a war allows boys to look like men. This seems a shallow benefit, but it is no small thing for a teenage boy to have something that yanks him out of his social floundering and places him, unlaughed at, in the company of heroes. While kidding around with the young PLO recruits in Rashidieh, and

101

later on as well, I noticed in myself a general tendency to treat these children with respect, more than I ever would American teenagers, perhaps because they had the sanction and capacity to kill. But it was not so much that I was afraid of them as that I saw they had committed themselves to the most dangerous game in the world and were visibly dignified by that commitment.

So is it valuable, then, this heightening, ennobling tradition that teaches the children of Rashidieh to leap over bonfires with guns in their arms, makes them more alert to each other's welfare, gives them pride and a sense of importance? No. It cannot be. The question was rhetorical from the start. For one thing, a state of war takes away the freedom of thought and opinion. It provides an ideology, all right, but only one, and individual disagreement is called treason or sedition. For another thing, all the virtues war encourages are almost always in the most simpleminded forms, the moral choices lying between stark extremes that require no imaginative shadings of one's own. War may be hell, but intellectually and spiritually war is also easy. That may be why it is resorted to so readily, why in fact children can do it so well.

Yet the overriding reason that war can never be deemed useful, whatever benefits are evident or concocted, is that war, like most things, cannot be judged outside its context. And the context of war is death. For all its elaborate emphases on order and discipline, the final purpose of war is to create chaos and ruin. Thus the enterprise is essentially a sham, not just a pretense of nobility and valor amid the cluster bombs and gas attacks, but a sham in the abstract. It entices one to virtue in the pursuit of vice, however necessary or justifiable. War is a moral lie. And all the good that accrues to children in a state of war is in the name of a moral lie.

Such a conclusion only made it more troubling to talk with Ahmed the following morning. Labadi introduces the boy as I wait in the PLO press office to learn whether the baby Palestine has been located and if I may see her. Labadi is still working on it. Meanwhile, would I not like to speak with Ahmed here? Ahmed is a leader in several PLO youth groups. At age fifteen he has already made speeches for the PLO in Cyprus, Egypt, East Germany, Czechoslovakia, Bulgaria, Cuba and Moscow. One PLO youth organization to which Ahmed belongs trains guerrillas from the ages of eight to sixteen, when they may graduate to the rank of full commando. The reason that Ahmed participates in several groups, explains Labadi, is that "he is so active, he doesn't want to let anything get past him." He raises a hint of a smile to let the boy know that he is teasing him. Ahmed smiles back broadly. His red beret rests precariously on a cushion of burgeoning hair. His eyes look both inquisitive and pained, quite soft for a promising soldier and propagandist.

Ahmed is sitting at the far end of a couch in a room at the rear of the building. On quiet days the routine of the PLO press office is to pass out public relations material, such as the baby Palestine postcard, and to display Israeli weapons recovered from air raids: a rocket with Hebrew lettering leaning against a corner; the contents of a cluster bomb lying in a helmet like a nest of brown eggs. This is not a quiet day. It is time to get things back in order after the car bombing. Labadi tries to catch up with his paperwork at a metal desk in the one room that is not overwhelmed by the noise of the cleanup. From time to time he looks up to see if Ahmed needs a clarification in translation. On the whole, Ahmed's English is excellent.

"I was a child in 1970 when the war began. Our family was thrown out of our house. We lived in a school for many days. Then we lived someplace else. Afterwards, we moved back to our house but were evicted again. Once the war started, every place was dangerous. No place seemed safer than another." Still, Ahmed says that he was not afraid, even at so young an age, because "I figured out that a man may only die once."

"How long do you think you will live?"

"No one can know. Maybe I'll die in a minute." (An unnerving crash of debris out on the balcony.)

He hopes to study medicine one day, "because my people

need doctors." Asked if he has a more personal impetus, he says that he loves science, and his expression shows it. "I love to see how the body works—the head, the stomach, the heart, the blood." Can he retain his politics and be a doctor too?

"The first work of a doctor is not to be a political man. His first work is to be a social man." He uses "social" in the wide, literal sense.

He is presented with a hypothetical situation: "You are a doctor fighting in Israel. A wounded Israeli comes to you for help. Are you a Palestinian or a doctor?"

"A doctor." No hesitation.

Ahmed is the youngest of seven children. His mother is Lebanese, his father Palestinian. He reads some, but not a great deal; his many duties give him little free time. He swims and plays soccer. He has a dreamy quality along with his surefootedness. I imagine that he has been chosen as a spokesman for PLO youth for his friendliness rather than any special gift of oratory. Sitting beneath the portrait of the sunglassed Arafat, he looks nothing like a demagogue.

"What is the most beautiful thing you have ever seen?"

"Palestinian soldiers. Because they defend our people."

"Have you ever seen something beautiful that is a bit more peaceful?"

"Yes." He smiles. "My lovely girl Jomaneh." Asked to describe this Jomaneh, he considers with only mild embarrassment. "She is not black and not white. Her eyes are green, I suppose. Her hair is long and blond."

"Is she intelligent?"

He turns to Labadi. "What should I tell him?"

"The truth."

"Yes, she is intelligent. But no girls are *very* intelligent. Jomaneh is more intelligent than most." Labadi smiles but does not look up.

"What is the saddest thing you have ever seen?"

"The sight of children without their parents," he says at once. In the Fakhani air raid last summer, the one in which

Palestine's mother was killed, Ahmed came upon three such children wandering dazed in the streets. He took them to his house, where they lived until a home was found for them. Ahmed did not talk with the children a great deal, because they were crying most of the time. Yes, he does indeed feel older than fifteen. "Because I do a job greater than myself."

He is asked if he believes in God. His "yes" is awed. Is his faith at all shaken when he sees the devastation of the wars, the devastation of yesterday's explosion, for example? "Do you think, How could God allow such a thing to happen?" His answer is like Elizabeth's in Belfast: "No. There is no relationship between God and the people who do such things. God does His work, man his."

I start to pose another question, but one of Labadi's assistants enters the room to curtail the interview. Ahmed is needed to participate in the funeral procession that is about to begin. Eddie and I will go along. It is a procession for Sami al-Ghoush, a leader of the PFLP who was killed in yesterday's bombing. Sami and his wife had just delivered their ten-year-old daughter Lara to school and were driving their car into Wafik Al Tibi Street at the precise moment the bomb exploded. Sami's wife was also killed, and she will be buried quietly in what the Palestinians call their "Martyrs Cemetery," where the graves are marked with large, framed photographs of the dead instead of headstones. This procession, however, is for Sami alone. He was an important political figure, and his funeral is a political event. Before Ahmed leaves to join the others, I ask him if he foresees peace at any time.

"I do not think the war will last forever," he says thoughtfully. "I will work for that day." We shake hands warmly for people who have only just met, neither of us suspecting that we will meet again in nine months, with the world about to change and no peace in sight.

Out on the street, Lara al-Ghoush, the only child of the slain parents, has been placed at the head of the procession to symbolize the effect of the bombing, and for a while she holds her ground with courage. She wears a brownish barrette in her white-blond hair, which has been parted in the middle and drawn to the back. Her dotted white dress has short puffed sleeves and a Peter Pan collar. It is well pressed. Clearly, Lara has been crying a great deal, but she is not crying now. Her eyes are hollowed with dark rings. If the girl were a dowager, you would say of her face: How beautiful it must have looked when she was young.

Then Lara breaks down again. She covers her forehead with her right hand, as if stricken with a headache. With the permission of the grown-ups, her companions lead her away to a metal chair in front of a store, where she rests as the procession begins to move without her. She rejoins it later at the rear, half-hidden behind the lines of PLO soldiers, and the antiaircraft guns, and the sound trucks blaring tinny martial music. Photographs of her father and mother are displayed in the windows of an ambulance that serves as a hearse. The red lights of the ambulance spin, the siren wails at a steady pitch, and the procession of some eight hundred Palestinians makes its mile-long journey through the dusty marketplace where chickens squawk in hanging cages and children clap at the parade. Now the children. Now the women in black. Now a bagpipe band, a legacy of the years of British rule.

The procession halts at a dirt clearing, where the crowd encircles a hoarse speaker:

"We are following the great leader who has been killed by the enemies." Sami's coffin has been removed from the ambulance and is borne by six soldiers in helmets. Their faces shine with sweat. The coffin is wood painted silver. At first it tilts and looks about to spill, the soldiers on one side holding it higher than the others, but immediately it is righted again and draped with the Palestinian flag. The crowd climbs mounds of earth around the speaker in order to see him better.

"He has been killed by the Phalangists and the Israelis and the CIA. Now we swear for his family: We will continue his mission. We may give up our soil, but not our weapons."

106

Lara is said to be nearby, but no one has seen her since the march began.

"I wonder what she is thinking?" I ask a soldier in the crowd.

"She is thinking, Get revenge."

At a roadblock on the way back to the Hotel Commodore, I find myself balking at yet another kid soldier's demand for my papers of identification. Most of my annoyance is due to the heat, I am sure, but I am not used to these impositions, and they do not grow on you. I realize that these identity searches must have their effects on the children as well: here, in Belfast, on the West Bank, or any place where soldiers command the streets. On the surface a checkpoint is merely a place where one is asked to identify himself for purposes of security. In essence, however, it is a moment when one must prove who he is; and in a way he must prove *that* he is. It is easily enough done, so there is nothing to fret about. Show your card and pass along. But a year or two or ten of someone challenging your existence every mile or so, or as in Beirut every thirty yards, or as in Belfast at the shifting mobile checkpoints that one morning might arise in front of your own door—what then? At first, one will depend on one's identity card for proof of existence, and then on the card examiners, on the cool-eyed guards who raise their arms like priests giving benediction, and stop you, and stand there at ease reading words with your life in them. After a few years they could remove the checkpoint entirely, and somewhere in your submerged desires you would beg them to stay. You are your own checkpoint.

This may be truer for grown-ups than for children, of course. For the children there is an element of game playing in this identity-card business too, just as there is in all facets of war making, and perhaps it is in some way comforting for a child to know that there are places on earth where he can prove without doubt who he is. But what happens when someone like Ahmed or Nabil eventually begins to think of himself as the person at the checkpoint? What happens when he realizes that safe prog-

107

ress is a rite of passage, and that he has been proceeding year by year into adulthood simply because he has been able to identify himself properly according to the standard of the roadblock? This is how freedoms go—not all at once in a flood, but in the slow heat and silence, the way beaches gradually disappear.

On a solitary walk that night I wander into a street in the area of the hotel where the lights have all gone out. Headlamps of passing cars make menacing shadows on the walls of buildings and on the billboards advertising movies. *Superman II* is coming to Beirut. Stumbling in the rubble, I come up face to face with a boy of twelve or so holding a machine gun at his waist. He looks terrified, as if I had just dropped in from the moon. Then, recovering his composure, he gestures for me to keep moving. In the hotel bar later on, a young woman reporter tells a table full of journalists about a detached human face that was found in a stairwell after the car bombing. She moves quite close to say this. Her eyes are moist and bright with excitement.

The following morning I prepare to leave for Athens for three days' rest. Eddie will stay on in Lebanon to take more pictures. As I pack, Labadi phones to say that he has located the baby Palestine. She is kept in a nursery in a nearby hospital while her father works during the days, and she is in that hospital right now. I have just enough time to get there before my flight, time to take one look at the famous child. Asam will meet me. In front of the Commodore I say good-bye to Abu Said, experiencing my only sincere regrets at leaving Beirut, feeling in fact quite lucky to be getting out with my limbs in place. Saleem says a charming, sheepish good-bye. We will all reconvene in nine months, and none of us knows it.

At the Akka Hospital I stand near the nursery wall as the baby is brought forward. She is dressed in a bright blue sleep suit with the words "Space Patrol" on the pocket, and she is laid, stomach up, on a small white mat. Struggling to raise her head, she falls back, whimpers momentarily, then tries again. Soft hairs fringe the triangle of her fontanel, like new shoots after a brush fire. I look her over for marks of her explosive birth, but I can see only a dark brown bruise on her right heel. The nurse tells us that Palestine was in intensive care for a long time, and that some surgery was done. The baby's blood had to be replaced twice totally. She looks fine, strong, not even especially small for her three months.

Now she rolls back and forth on the mat. Her legs, still bowed, kick out spasmodically. In order to gain her attention the nurse brings out a birdcage and places it beside the baby. For a moment Palestine seems pleased by the two jumpy canaries, one black, one yellow. Now she looks bored again. I cannot tell if she hears the music in the nursery or the murmurs of the other babies stacked up in their double-decker box cribs. She acknowledges no one. Asam whispers that I must hurry if I am to make my plane. Palestine is sleeping now, her arms fallen at her sides, her eyes like dark crescents on her placid face. The grown-ups in the room are staring at her as if looking for a sign. There is no sign.

FIVE

Pausing with
Telemachos

Where have I been so far? What has been told me? By the time
I set down in Athens I had been traveling a mere three weeks,
but it seemed much longer than that, in part because of the distances covered and the novelty and variety of things seen, in
part because I was lonely. Unaccustomed to travel, I did not realize how deep and severe a sense of separation it creates, how
much like death it is. All those expressions one hears connecting death with taking a journey suddenly seemed plausible to
me. Wife and children behind; friends and job behind; house
and possessions and all familiar sights receding from one's
touch, as if at the end of a dock, their absence intensified by the
presence of the strange and foreign. If taking a journey is akin
to death, then it is death with both heaven and hell involved.
Up to this point, I had experienced, most often, a mounting ex-
hilaration at the discoveries and surprises, no matter how heartbreaking the information. Yet there was a good deal of emotional sinking as well, the feeling of being sucked into the earth,
of having lost all moorings and orientation. I felt that I had
been gone a long time, but also that I was moving too fast.

For the next three days in Athens, then, I would try to set some things in order. I wanted to rest and to wander among the sights like any first-time tourist, but also to think about what I had seen and to assess what the children were saying. I would wind up visiting just two places besides the Acropolis: the Temple of Poseidon at Sounion, and Mount Lycabettus. The rest of the time I would spend taking long, purposeless walks in the city and swimming in the pool of a hotel near my own. Athens was hot and noisy; I did not expect it. It was especially noisy that October because of the upcoming national elections. Every evening Syntagma Square was blazing white, lit up by enormous spotlights mounted on trucks, the kind used for movie premiers. The candidates' speeches were amplified ferociously and roared through the city.

At night I would sit on the small stone balcony of the Grande Bretagne Hotel and listen to the speakers promoting themselves in a language I could not understand. They were unmistakable as politicians, nonetheless. The tones, the cadences, the mixture of studied sobriety and exhortation. I thought of Pericles speaking to the parents of the dead after the wars with Sparta. Knowing next to nothing about modern Greece, I found that I often fell back on what little more I remembered about the ancients. From my balcony after dark I stared across the square at the Parthenon, illuminated harshly like any modern public building. Then I saw it as it must have been at night in the fifth century B.C., not illuminated, its solemn darkness poised protectively above the city like a watchdog.

Interesting, how much the mind can take in in a single sweep, how much past and present, dream and fact. No wonder it works so hard to achieve generalities. Nothing else tests its ingenuity, since as a mere collecting machine its capacity is probably infinite. My problem now, after three weeks on the road, was to search for generalities, to unconfuse the voices of the children as I replayed them in my mind. Eventually, I came up with three things, three common strains that cut across their

112

differences of age, sex, temperament, circumstances and nationality. The first was tone; the second, theme; the third, belief.

Basically, the children's tone was the sound of an attitude, one of great seriousness, an attitude displayed in its simplest form by their rapt attentiveness to questions, however casually put, and the careful, scrupulous way they gave their answers. One has to allow a little for the odd presence of the reporter who, as a social figure, always seems to command attention beyond his station, simply because he is openly recording what people are saying, and is an undisguised threat to publish it. But children generally do not worry about the effects of publicity, and these particular children, while they may have been somewhat surprised by a foreigner swooping down on their lives, showed no uneasiness whatever and never a sign of embarrassment.

Nor did any of them play the wise guy or the fool or collapse in howls and giggles the way any kid reasonably might when confronted with so solemn a subject. Not once. Not once did they show normal signs of frivolity. The closest I came to seeing self-absorption in any of the children was on the West Bank in El Bireh, when a six-year-old named Hilda was asked by her teacher to sing a Palestinian song for Eddie and me. This clearly was Hilda's moment. She carried a red checkered purse that matched her red checkered dress, and as she mounted the little chair on which she had decided to perform, her smile enveloped the assembled. Then she sang, all six long verses of the song, and bathed lavishly in the ensuing applause. It was loud and devoted, befitting a star.

Even Hilda's showmanship belied a fundamental formality. All the children had this sort of natural stature. It made no difference if they were as relatively free in their situations as the Israeli children and the Palestinian children in Lebanon, or as bottled up as the Palestinians on the West Bank, or if, as the Irish, they were somewhere in the middle. Every one of the children I had talked with so far displayed what one often calls a sense of the occasion. But what occasion? The only event they had in common was war. It might be that their attitude of formality was a tacit assertion against war, a polite little protest against the mayhem around them. But this seemed too easy and untrue. Their sense of the occasion felt deeper than that, reflecting not something they perceived in the world but in themselves. The tone they had in common was the sound of their lives.

The theme these children shared was that of revenge. When in Belfast Joseph turned to Paul and urged the spirit of revenge on his friend, he was striking that theme, which was to crop up within each country on the journey. For Joseph the course of revenge was clear, in one direction. For Paul, Bernadette and Elizabeth it seemed equally clear in the opposite direction, as it did for Keith and Heather as well. Elizabeth did not at all sound helpless when asked if she sought vengeance for the killings in her family. Her answer, "Against whom?" dismissed the idea outright.

In the north of Israel, Hadara's reaction to the idea of vengeance was conciliation, and Nimrod's "What good is this revenge?" indicated a real conviction in him. Dror shared that conviction. Like Joseph, the two teenage girls in Qiryat Shemona tended the other way, as did Waffa, the Palestinian girl in Ramallah whose father had been thrown in jail. But in another part of the West Bank, the girl Hania, who was shot in the leg by Israeli soldiers, declared: "I would not shoot them. Even if I had had a gun at the time, I could not." Her friend Nabil, angry as he was, expressed the same feelings. Even among the Palestinian children in Lebanon, where the ideal of revenge took on a mythic size, the actual war whoops came from the grown-ups, whereas for children like Jamila, Mona and Boutros the idea was subsumed and mollified in talk of historical destiny and historical justice. Ahmed never mentioned the word revenge. Lara had it spoken for her.

One added element in this casual survey is that the children who were most vehement about getting even with their enemies had the least to be vengeful about. Waffa's father was thrown in jail, and while that could hardly be called an insignificant injury, it could not compare to what was suffered by Paul Rowe or by Boutros or by any of the others whose parents' lives had been taken. This, as General Sherman pointed out in his "War is hell" speech, is the way of the world, of course. Those who have suffered least in a war are usually the loudest in its advocacy, the truism evidently applying at an early age.

But for the great majority of the children seen so far, it was revenge that stood for hell, and they would have none of it. Here, then, was a consensus, but an odd one. If the guiding presence of adults is as important to children as it is said to be, why were not these particular children moved toward the vengeance the grown-ups promoted? How could they resist it? In terms of their own behavior the institution of revenge ought to make good sense to these children, for all the familiar reasons of standing up for one's rights, of not allowing oneself to be stepped on continually, of pride and honor and so forth. To be sure, they would be told in school and church that vengeance is the Lord's, but in the ordinary practice of their lives, it should seem fairly natural to seek redress for the wrongs done them. If revenge is not exactly sweet, it should at least hold a certain demonstrable satisfaction. Yet they forbore.

The remarkable thing is that this forbearance occurred in atmospheres where the idea of revenge would seem to be peculiarly fitting. Francis Bacon called revenge "a kind of wild justice," by which one assumes he meant that it takes the place of tame and ordinary justice. Thus the idea of revenge stands out as especially savage and stupid in places where established systems of justice, courts and the like, remain intact. But in situations like war zones, where few such systems prevail, and where all hell breaking loose is the order of the day, what could be more appropriate and normal than wild justice? In short, the adults who urged the spirit of revenge on the children not only had rudimentary logic on their side, but the visible circumstances of the world as well. If a child could not pick up the

115

idea of an eye for an eye under such conditions, he must be uneducable.

I wondered if the small appeal this idea held for the children had anything to do with the fact that as a human prerogative revenge always seems a bit fanciful, a pretense. Not that there is no revenge taking in the real world; only that when it happens it shows itself to be less an act of retaliation than one of pure violence. Anyone who tries it usually experiences more sorrow than vindication, and instead of being overwhelmed with regenerated power, winds up feeling sapped and futile. George Orwell once described a prisoner-of-war camp in southern Germany just after the war, when he was being given a tour by a Jewish soldier from Vienna who had been hired by the American army to help with the interrogation of prisoners. As the guide showed Orwell around, he pointed out a former SS officer, disheveled, asleep in the mud, a sight of disgust to Orwell. The guide kicked the man and forced him to stand at attention. Another SS officer they came upon was humiliated verbally. Orwell concluded that the Jewish soldier, however impassioned he tried to make himself, derived no pleasure from these acts, that, as he said, "the whole idea of revenge and punishment is a childish daydream." So it usually appears. In prospect, the picture of striking back at one's enemies is uplifting, in its way delightful, but at the moment the act occurs all the drama fades, and one is simply left with the desire to do harm.

Perhaps this is yet another reason that Hamlet waited so long to decide what to do. There was a child of war surely, the son addressed by the dead father at the outset of the story, calling upon his boy to swear to avenge him so that he the ghost could rest in peace. As long as Hamlet put off the act, it was all right, this idea of revenge. Ennobling, it made for fine long speeches, lively scenes, and above all, tragedy. When the bodies finally lay on the stage, however, *Hamlet* was no longer tragic, it was pathetic, just as Ahab was pathetic when he finally harpooned his enemy, and Heathcliff and Achilles and all the rest. In that same essay about the POW camp, Orwell told of a woman who fired five shots into the hanging body of the dead Mussolini, declaring, "Those are for my five sons!" If the anecdote is true, her gesture was a perfect metaphor for the empty joys of getting even.

Still, if the essence of revenge resides in the imagination, it would seem all the more likely for the kids to embrace the idea. All children take to fantasies, and these were no different. The Irish girls had their romantic novels, the Israeli children enjoyed a popular series of adventure books akin to the Hardy Boys and Nancy Drew mysteries, and the children I met everywhere devoured the usual ration of cartoon and comic book supermen. One might think that the fantasy of revenge cooperated so nicely with the realities of the children's daily experiences, it would be impossible to turn down. They did so nonetheless. They did so actively, despite the pressures from above and all the natural temptations of their lives.

At the same time, the idea of revenge did not seem to be replaced in their minds with the idea of forgiveness. Psychologists sometimes note that forgiveness is itself a form of revenge, since the heaping of virtue upon the head of one's enemy is bound to bring him low. One keeps one's vice and expels it too. Yet as most people will attest, there is such a thing as genuine unalloyed forgiveness in the world. Nor is it necessary to be a saint to feel it. If nothing else, the act of forgiving those who trespass against us provides a holiday from petty anxieties and is therefore a practical decision, little different from relieving a headache.

These children, on the other hand, did not forgive their enemies, or at least they gave no such sign. Rather, the absence of a desire for vengeance in them seemed to be just that, an absence. Both Nimrod and Hania expressed their opposition to revenge solely in the negative. They replaced revenge with nothing, nor did they or any of the others suggest any moral framework whatever in which their enemies ought properly to be regarded, beyond specific criticisms for specific wrongs: "They took our land." Why did they not react more vividly to the murderousness around them? Passive resistance? Possibly. Yet their resistance, if this is what it was, did not seem passive, but based on other grounds.

If this attitude of theirs was evident to someone like me, making a fast-moving inquiry, surely it must have been obvious to the grown-ups who live with these children all the time. Did they feel at all frustrated by the lack of a vengeful spirit displayed by their young, or did they simply treat this absence as one would other absences in children, as gaps to be filled by careful and steady instruction? "They are so young," said Colonel Azmi, "but they are so proud." I pictured life at home at the Azmis, the dinner table catechisms in which Samer's performances improved by the week. Azmi was no fool. Whatever he might say about the pride of youth, he must have seen the silliness of trying to burn vengeance into his four-year-old son. Yet he persisted, perhaps feeling that it was only a matter of time before the words became dogma, before Samer would at last understand that his ritual could be applied to life. "My son will carry my gun," said Azmi. Certainly he had history on his side.

At Sounion, on my second day in Greece, I stood between two pillars of the Temple of Poseidon thinking of Odysseus and Telemachos and of their own parable of revenge. Below and all around me the Aegean lay like a rippled sheet of blue fabric, at once motionless and rolling. On this wide water Odysseus rode home to Ithaca and to the son who awaited his guidance on how to handle Penelope's suitors. Odysseus' solution was characteristically simple. Telemachos responded, amazed, "O Father, all my life your fame as a fighting man has echoed in my ears—your skill with weapons and the tricks of war—but what you speak of is a staggering thing, beyond imagining for me." (Robert Fitzgerald's translation.)

At an earlier point in the poem, before Odysseus returns, Telemachos is preparing to call a meeting of the council of Ithaca. Homer describes the scene this way: "And when Rosy-fingered Dawn appeared, the child of morn, the dear son of Odysseus, rose from his bed and put on his garments." The passage is deliberately beautiful. I wondered if Homer was making a point in two such different passages, comparing Telemachos as he was on his own with Telemachos under his father's tutelage. Perhaps not. That was another world. The sun that filled Sounion with light was understood by Homer to be a golden disk. Still, Telemachos, like the other children of war, had to be prodded toward the "staggering thing." I wondered what his thoughts were all those long days when Odysseus had not yet returned, waiting on a promontory like Sounion and searching the sea for the man who would shape his life.

If all this were so, if in fact the children in the war zones did not take naturally to the idea of revenge and had to be coaxed to it by their elders, was it possible that revenge is purely an adult invention? I was not thinking about the daydreams of revenge which, being as childish as Orwell called them, fill children's minds readily and all the time. But the facts of revenge, the actual plottings, the planning of attacks, the bombings and beheadings—they are way beyond the scope of children. Of course, this may be explained away as merely a matter of power. Telemachos might have meant that he could not imagine slaughtering the suitors as a statement of practicality, not morals, and given the Homeric ideal of hero-as-warrior, that is most likely what he did mean. Yet the children I was speaking with did not abjure revenge because they could not achieve it but because it seemed to hold no attractiveness for them. Adults, on the other hand, spoke quite well of it. Children grow up. At what point in their growing up did revenge become attractive to them, and for what reasons?

It was not, after all, as if the penalties for taking revenge were ever obscured. All around them in Northern Ireland, Israel and Lebanon children could see plainly the consequences of continually striking back. If there was a core to the appeal of taking revenge, it could not be anything rational. Odysseus himself made no pretense that the elimination of the suitors would clear up the mess in Ithaca. To the contrary; he anticipated and predicted the blood feud that was bound to follow the slaughter of those who were the finest young men of the country, and he said so to his son. Yet revenge was the solution he advocated.

The more one thought of it, the more preposterous it became. Revenge was destructive to the personality, corrosive to one's morals, utterly useless as a political weapon; therefore, it was promoted. Since at some moment in their maturing lives the children adopted this bad idea as their own, they did so in spite of its patent absurdity. Perhaps it was a question of tradition, a way of honoring history by keeping up the old customs. Or perhaps, and this is what seemed dismaying, they adopted the idea of revenge simply because it was a sure sign of adulthood, because, unreasonable and debilitating though it may be, the exercise of vengeance offered concrete proof that they were at last entitled to the world of men.

Revenge could thus be thought of as a family gift, an heirloom passed down the generations. Could you not see it—Odysseus heading home, or Colonel Azmi heading home, or Joseph's father and all the fathers and mothers of the Irish, the Palestinians and the Israelis, bearing with them this strange device which would serve as a gate to adulthood? In order for a child to grow up in these war zones, he must be prepared to assume this mark of continuity. Before then he would have to be shown how grown-up an idea it was, and this by example, an example set by his parents railing against their enemies in his presence, the example of their sputtering fury at their own impotence, their checked desires to cut down all, and the sons and the granddaughters of all who ever did their people injury.

A picture was beginning to come clear here, one that had started dimly to take shape in Belfast and which had grown steadily sharper in each country as I went eastward. I began to realize that most of the children in the war zones patronized their parents. Gently and with much solicitude, they did so. I believed that they tolerated things in their parents, like the idea of revenge, which they did not accept in the abstract or for themselves, and that they did so either because they loved their parents, which they truly did, and this acceptance was a way of showing it, or because they had small choice in the matter. To some extent, children always patronize their parents as a means of survival. A grown-up rants irrationally; a child grows very still. But war has a way of elevating our irrationalities to magnificent heights. It occurred to me the children recognized this madness, feared it, and felt superior to it all at once. In short, they loved their parents, but they did not believe in them.

They did, however, believe in God. And they believed quite strongly. This was the third common strain among the children. What in fact they must have seen in their parents' howling for vengeance was essentially a rage against God, since revenge always implies that God's justice is too slow and circuitous. If God could be counted on to knock off the Taigs, Prods, Jews and Arabs, then human bloodletting would be unnecessary. Since God was unreliable in this regard, grown-ups would have to do the work for Him. It was another way of saying that the adults were of little faith, or at any rate that their faith was modified to suit their needs.

But the faith of the children seemed abiding and boundless. I don't know why this surprised me, since faith is often intensified in dangerous situations, yet the attitudes of these children seemed to transcend immediate causes. When Bernadette and Elizabeth declared their trust in God in spite of everything falling down around them, they did not sound as if they had gone through any arduous process of reaffirmation but rather that they accepted, willingly and easily, the mystery of God as it is. "At first," Elizabeth said, "I couldn't understand why this was all happenin' to us." Then she dismissed the question, not as profane but beside the point.

So too Ahmed, responding to the same question about the endurance of his faith after the car bombing, said, "God does His work, man his." He was assured, convinced. Even Hadara's poem challenging the beneficence of God gained its strength from the fact that the girl was going through spiritual turmoil in the open. Fleeing God, she gave every sign she would wind up succumbing.

Presumably, the initial sources of this faith were the families of the children. If the elders did not by their own example promote belief in God, they undoubtedly did so like families anywhere, through custom and habit. A good Catholic, Moslem, Protestant or Jew was supposed to believe in God, and so would his children. Besides, God could always be outfitted for battle, as in the IRA murals in Belfast with Jesus portrayed as a hunger striker. The parents did not have to really believe. If they had lost their faith, or if they recognized in themselves the attitudes and behavior that made their faith seem hypocritical, then perhaps they urged faith on their children out of feelings of guilt. Either way, their children would be growing up in nominally religious homes, with the proper tracts on the walls and the appropriate ceremonies observed even though the wolves might be on both sides of the door.

Still, one sensed that the source of their faith was not parental but rather something generated by themselves for themselves. They did not say so. They simply seemed to take for granted the vast chasm between the world of experience and the world of faith, between reason and belief, as if the mystery of God only achieved its power in proportion to its distance from cause-and-effect arguments. God does His work, man his. This decision to believe had to take an enormous act of will, because the reality of God, much less the benevolence of God, could hardly be proved by the explosive life around them. It is as if the children understood on their own that above everything else God required this decision to believe in Him without rational bases. Having made that decision, they could accept anything, including their own irrational surroundings.

Whatever the individual sources of their faith, it was their sincerity that bound these children to one another. Protestants, Catholics, Jews, Moslems, they each seemed to feel some personal tie to God, a special guardianship. It struck me that on this journey I would be coming in contact with practically all the major religions of the world, and that there might be vast differences of spiritual context when the subject of faith came up. Yet when these children spoke of their particular God, one did not see the God of the Moslems or of the Jews or of the Irish Catholics hovering over certain designated neighborhoods of Belfast. Rather, there emerged the image of a single, comprehensive God for children in these particular straits, a God of the children of war, whose constituency had needs and fears like none other, offered prayers like none other, whose emergencies and doubts were theirs alone.

Was this special deity the source of the tone they shared as well? Was the occasion of which they showed a sense that of their own piety? It was quite possible, I thought, that all the children would be seeing the same God. They were seeing the same world, fundamentally, the same wounds and cruelty. They were hearing the same political speeches. They were being given the same rationales, the same calls to arms. They were used for the same things and cherished for the same purposes, and when their friends and parents were shot to death, they would be standing over the same graves with the same heads bowed toward the same fresh earth. Why would they not look to the same heaven, then? Where else was there to look? And looking, who else would they envisage but the particular God who could sit beside their particular hearts and tell them what no other elder would: that it was all right not to hate?

These three commonalities were linked, then; that seemed likely. The seriousness of attitude, the absence of revenge, the belief in God; each element drew some power from the other. This was by no means all that the children were made of, but it was something, the beginning of a definition. After three days in Athens I was on my way to a generality. That was encouraging. Yet if certain things were disentangled, certain others lay untouched upon. There was a core here, I knew it. I had glimpsed a part, but no more. In Asia I would get a bit further, by way of hell, but by the middle of the journey I still had more than halfway to go.

123

My last afternoon in Athens I climbed Mount Lycabettus, pulling my way up the dirt slopes by grasping bushes and saplings. The sun was about to turn pink when I arrived at the top and stood with my fellow tourists just beneath St. George's Chapel. Directly below lay the wealthiest roofs in the city. This is the highest spot on the Attic Plain, 886 feet up, and well above the Acropolis. In fact, Mount Lycabettus would have been selected over the site of the Acropolis as the place for the city's fortress, but the earliest Greeks did not possess the weapons necessary to secure that steep a hill, so Lycabettus remained unfortified all these years, serving mainly as a destination for tourists and as a place of worship. At midnight every Easter there is a Resurrection service in the chapel, after which thousands of Athenians who have gathered near the chapel wall begin a slow descent of the hill, each bearing a candle. First, the chapel is made totally dark, to suggest the tomb of Jesus. Then the priest comes forward, proclaiming "Christ is risen!" and the congregation ignites its candles, each celebrant taking the flame from the one behind him before the procession spirals downward in a chain of light.

I looked over at the Acropolis, then directly below at frantic modern Athens, easily grasping thousands of years of history in a single view. Up here the politicians' electrified voices came through as whispers, and the tourists rarely spoke, content to examine the spaces and distances. "Beyond the last peaks and all the seas of the world," lies Plato's Republic of "the fair and immortal children of the mind." So one is told. I suspected not. The serene republic felt a good deal closer to me just then, a place I had seen before and would see again, located approximately where I was standing.

SIX

Cambodia

The road to Khao I Dang is a looping highway extending from Bangkok east southeast 150 miles to the Thai-Cambodian border. At the town of Chachasongse we are halfway to the camp. The sun is barely up, a slice of gold light on the black horizon, but the area is already busy. Delivery trucks bulging with rice are parked in long lines on the shoulders of the highway waiting like patient animals for the hour when they are permitted to proceed into Bangkok. Schoolchildren in blue and white uniforms assemble at bus stops built in the form of doll-size pagodas. Cars pass our taxi wearing dabs of white clay and gold foil at the tops of their windshields. This, Matthew explains, indicates that Buddhist monks have blessed the vehicle. Socua adds that the blessing involves an elaborate ceremony in which the new owner of an automobile takes his prize to a Buddhist temple, a wat, to be consecrated and protected. The monks tie flowers to the grills. Matthew notes that the Thais wash their cars here by the roadside where their ancestors washed their elephants.

Schumann plays on the tape deck. Matthew Naythons, the *Time* photographer who will be with me in Thailand and in Hong Kong, has thought to bring cassettes along so that we may have Schumann on the way to the refugee camp. By now I have come to expect this sort of resourcefulness of Matthew. In two brief days in Bangkok he managed to set up meetings for us with most of the people who work with the Cambodian children in Khao I Dang, Saceo and the other camps; he discovered Socua and persuaded her to accompany us as an interpreter; he hired a taxi to drive us to Khao I Dang; and when the driver failed to show at four in the morning, he hired another on the spot. While running around Bangkok, Matthew also found the time to collect a pot of money from a betting pool he unknowingly won over a year before. A bartender held the cash, assuming that Matthew would be returning to Bangkok sooner or later.

Until two days ago everything I had heard of my prospective companion gave me the willies. Matthew is trained not as a photographer but a physician who in fact once worked as a medic in the Cambodian camps but now only practices infrequently because, I was told, he finds photography more exciting. He was supposed to meet me on the midnight flight from Athens, but he decided to take an extra day's holiday, loafing and sailing among the Greek islands. Neither of these signs of the playboy would have been especially troubling were it not for the additional item that earlier in the summer Matthew had been named *Cosmopolitan* magazine's "Bachelor of the Month." In short, my heart sank at the thought of Matthew Naythons, and when I first appraised him in the lobby of the Hotel Oriental and beheld his safari jacket and Pancho Villa mustache, it sank some more.

My impression was mostly wrong. Matthew loves the high life, all right, but he is no wild man. Once he casually saved my life in Hong Kong by pointing out that the antimalaria pills which I had been taking every day instead of once a week (I had forgotten the prescription) would, if I did not correct my

126

schedule, give me a disease so rare I might expect to make the medical journals. Whether or not he preferred the excitement of photography to medicine, Matthew must be a very good doctor indeed. In the towns along the road to Khao I Dang, proprietors of restaurants greeted him exuberantly with "Dr. Matthew!" in part because Matthew eats like a horse, albeit epicurean, in part because when he worked here as a medic he earned a reputation for kindness and tirelessness.

Not tireless for the moment, Matthew snoozes in the backseat, and Socua assumes the task of telling me about the region. Socua is herself Khmer. She prefers the term "Khmer" to "Cambodian," as do her countrymen, yet they also prefer "Cambodia" to "Kampuchea," since that is the name Pol Pot gave the country after his takeover in April 1975. Wherever possible, they seek to draw a distinction between the peaceful, dignified people once known as the Khmer and the murderers who called themselves the Khmer Rouge. Socua is in her mid-twenties, self-confident, attractive, her black hair cut short like a flapper's. A refugee herself, she lived and studied in San Francisco, and only recently came to Thailand to work with other refugees. Because of the war between the Khmer Rouge and the invading Vietnamese, travel to her homeland is impossible. She tells me that most of the people in Khao I Dang would also prefer to return home rather than be dispersed abroad.

For the present hope of returning is out of the question. The Vietnamese and Khmer Rouge are stalking each other in the jungles, leaving the innocent majority of Khmer terrorized, helpless and starving. The Thais, suffused with traditional hatred of the Vietnamese and with traditional contempt for the Khmer, sell weapons to the Khmer Rouge. These are largely U.S. weapons. I discover that my country is in the idiotic and shameful position of recognizing the Khmer Rouge in the UN, arming them in the jungles, and accepting their victims as refugees. As a sidelight to the Cambodian war, the Thai government does nothing to restrain the Thai pirates from raping and slaughtering the Vietnamese boat people, including children, whose junks stray into Thai waters. Later in Hong Kong I read of a thirteen-year-old Vietnamese girl raped over and again by Thai pirates who passed her around. In seven days aboard the West German rescue ship she did not smile once. The nurses wept when they first saw her.

On a map one can see how close these now famous nations are—Thailand, Laos, Viet Nam, Cambodia—pressed together as tightly as four midwestern American states. The Thais first won independence from the Khmer in 1238. It has taken a while to hone these enmities.

In Bangkok I dined with a Thai journalist who, when I asked him what life was like in camps like Khao I Dang, answered blithely: "They fuck and smoke dope." Perhaps he was merely trying to talk tough, the way journalists sometimes do with one another in order to establish objectivity. But his attitude toward the refugees was common among the Thais. The Khmer were not wanted in Thailand. Their presence was tolerated because the UN, through the United Nations High Commissioner on Refugees (UNHCR), set up the refugee camps, maintained them, and in so doing brought money into the country. What nettled the Thais, however, was the thought that the Khmer might remain and eventually intermingle, an idea evidently so abhorrent that no one whom I consulted on the subject doubted for an instant that the Thai government would gladly deliver the refugees in the camps back to the Khmer Rouge whenever such a move seemed expedient. Later, the children of Khao I Dang would tell me they anticipated such a thing and would point to Khao I Dang Mountain, a large, craggy hill hunched over the camp, on whose crest they imagined the Khmer Rouge soldiers gathering in the night, preparing to hurtle noiselessly down into their huts.

Where we are driving now, Socua says, looks a great deal like Cambodia. The land is flat, the sky heaving with blue clouds streaked yellow and white. Rice fields lie sodden on either side of the highway, which crosses the klongs, the canals, raised unusually high by last night's downpour. The road itself is flooded in spots, the toads and eels floating out of the klongs with the rain. From the water rise the stems of lotus flowers, the lotus serving as the symbol of Buddhism because it emerges from the mud to become something beautiful. The symbolism of the flower is divided among stages of growth, each stage simulating the advancement of a man's virtue. At the lowest level, still resting on the mud, is one who regards life as its own end. Midway up is the man who concedes he has much to learn. The tallest lotus is he who has risen above the water level and is now prepared to become a bodhisattva, to achieve the serenity of Buddha.

"Cobras lie in these rice paddies," says Matthew, waking cheerily. "Villagers call them 'three-step snakes.' One bite, three steps and you're dead." He changes the tape to Pachelbel.

Many of the houses rest on stilts here. Socua tells me that in Cambodia the height of one's house signifies how rich and important he is. The height of a house is often increased by piling roof upon roof. "If one wishes to determine how powerful you are, he will not ask directly, which would be rude. He will ask instead how many roofs your house has." At least that was so when Cambodia still had gradations of self-esteem. That is gone now, Socua says. War has changed her people. A country known for centuries for docility, gentleness and pride—"known mainly for smiling"—is ravaged now, the people shaken, their former values ruined and cast away. "Still, you will see vestiges of the old dignity in Khao I Dang. Whenever parents want to discipline their children, all they do is remind them: "You are Khmer. Behave like Khmer." From a very early age, Socua says, the children are taught to honor, in this order, the land, the nation, their dead ancestors, their parents, their village, including their friends. "They continue to do so, even in a place like Khao I Dang."

We stop for gas at a two-pump station where children rush toward us and attack the taxi with their wash rags. Child labor is still plentiful in Thailand. Before us a water buffalo ambles by, giving a lift to a small perky bird. I breathe in the thick, sweet air of Asia, to which I am now somewhat accustomed, and watch the sky go first dark then white in quick succession. My mind swims between quietude and apprehension. It has done so for a day or two. One evening at the Hotel Oriental I watched the lights from the hotel dock wriggle in the Chao Phraya River, which runs beside the hotel, the lights imitating the undulation of the water but not synchronized with it. So I felt in this region.

What made me particularly apprehensive was my conversation with the Geretys the night before last. Pierce Gerety is director of the International Rescue Committee in Thailand; his wife Marie is coordinator of the children's program of the IRC. Meeting with Matthew and me in the Oriental, they told us we must be prepared to hear stories of absolute horror from the children, that some of those who managed to escape from the Khmer Rouge emerged with the kinds of experiences no Westerner can comprehend. Marie said that there were older children in the Saceo camp who had served as soldiers for the Khmer Rouge. Some informed on their parents, who were then executed. Some children did the killing themselves. They have now returned to their jungle, Marie told us, but while in the camp they neither laughed nor cried.

At Khao I Dang there are no known Khmer Rouge soldiers among the children, but the experiences related are as terrible. The Geretys urged me to find Neil Boothby when we got to Khao I Dang. Neil, a child psychologist from Harvard, has been working with the children at the camp for the past three months. He could tell me stories about the children I would not believe, that I would fervently wish not to believe. "The death toll is fantastic," said Pierce. "The cruelty incredible. You have to realize that their whole country has been burned over."

"Take a look at the drawings the children do," said Marie. "You'll see people tied to trees, pregnant women with Pol Pot's soldiers driving bayonets into their stomachs."

"Or people with their livers being cut out," Pierce added.

130

"One of Pol Pot's favorite tortures was to pluck out someone's liver with a specially devised hook. The victim could survive a full twenty minutes in that condition."

"Ask Neil to tell you the story of Peov." Marie spelled the name for me, but pronounced it "Po." The Geretys then proceeded to tell me the story themselves, about an eight-year-old girl now in Khao I Dang who drew a perplexing picture when she first arrived in the camp and did not speak for a full year. The Geretys described the drawing to me and then explained its meaning, which the girl Peov eventually revealed. I would meet this little girl. I was afraid to meet her.

Joseph Conrad lived at the Hotel Oriental for a while. A restaurant there is called Lord Jim. After talking with the Geretys, I thought instead of *Heart of Darkness* and realized I was headed there.

On the road again we pass a farm of trees standing at attention like an orchestra before a performance, and then a cluster of tombstones on sale near the town of Plaeng No. The land is hilly now, studded with boulders. This is where the Thai Army has established its main line of defense. We are within range of Vietnamese artillery, Matthew tells us, about eighteen to twenty kilometers from the Cambodian border. That night I heard the war thud in the distance like a muted drum. Near the town of Aranyaprathet we stop briefly to pick up our passes from the local commander so that we may proceed into Khao I Dang. A toothy Colonel Kitti greets my colleague: "Ah, Dr. Matthew! In another guise these days." Matthew and the colonel needle each other while Kitti signs the passes. "For Khao I Dang only." The colonel explains that there is talk of poisoned water in the other camps. He may be lying. Foreign journalists are not popular in Thailand these days because of stories exposing the Thai pirates.

In the middle of the morning on October 13, we arrive in Khao I Dang, swarmed immediately by small girls calling "Buy, please, buy," and selling wooden birds on wooden perches. Socua guides us through the children. She points to a

131

huddle of Khmer adults waiting by the gate to be moved in trucks to other camps. Their faces are lifeless. At its largest Khao I Dang held over 120,000 refugees. That population is reduced to 40,000 now, a number that sounds more manageable, given the small-town size of the camp, about seventy square acres. Behind the neat rows of straw-roofed huts rises the mountain Khao I Dang, or "spotted bitch mountain" or simply "spotted mountain"; evidently it translates both ways. Socua leads Matthew and me along Phnom Penh Road, a mud path named to recall the homeland of the Khmer. Their camp looks like an ancient village to me. Women in *sampots* skitter by with naked babies riding on their hips. Monks in yellow gowns sit cross-legged on long bamboo tables, their shaved heads lowered in contemplation. We arrive on a holiday, the last days of the Buddhist Lent. Everyone smiles at us openly, the children tagging along. Some are in tatters. I find them astonishingly beautiful.

"They think you'll take them home with you," says Socua. "Take care to say nothing that would indicate you might."

Neil Boothby greets us at the Children's Center, a long, dirt-floor hut the size of a mess hall in an army camp. We wired Neil from Bangkok to say why we were coming. He has already engaged an interpreter for us. Socua is thus free to work elsewhere in the camp. She will arrange a dance performance by the children later in the day. Our interpreter, Khav Yuom, called Yuom, is a man so small and fresh-faced he could pass for a child himself. In fact, I take him for a teenager until I look at him more earnestly. Yuom is in his mid-twenties. Partly because he looks like a boy, he not only managed to escape from the Khmer Rouge himself but to smuggle his wife and mother out of the country as well. He goes to get Ty Kim Seng, a ten-year-old who also escaped Pol Pot's soldiers and who arrived at Khao I Dang about a year ago. Ty Kim Seng is one of several children Neil has lined up for me to meet, the girl Peov being the last on the list. "She may not talk," he advises me.

"But Ty Kim Seng should respond quite well. He always

talked fairly freely, even when he first came to the camp and looked like this." Neil slides a sheet of paper toward me across the kitchen table where we sit. It is a crayon drawing of a bright orange skeletal figure with a grim mouth in an open frown. Round teardrops fall from the skeleton's eyes. Ty Kim Seng drew this picture shortly after he arrived at Khao I Dang. It refers to the time when the boy was eight and was forced to join one of the mobile work teams instituted by Pol Pot for the Khmer children's "education and well-being." When Ty Kim Seng first walked down into Khao I Dang, he was nearly dead from malnutrition.

No longer. Ty Kim Seng enters the hut alongside Yuom and greets me with a *wai,* a small bow of homage in which one's hands are pressed together as if in prayer and raised to one's face, the finger tips stopping at about eye level. I return the gesture, asking Yuom with my eyes if I have done the *wai* correctly. I soon realize he would never risk discourtesy by telling me if I erred. Yuom and Ty Kim Seng take the bench on the opposite side of the kitchen table, and we begin to talk above the squeals of the children outside the hut. The boy is visible to the middle of his chest. He wears a white sport shirt. His face is bright brown, his head held in balance by a pair of ears a bit too large for the rest. The effect is scholarly, not comical. He reminds me of Nimrod in Israel, although there is little actual resemblance. Something about the attitude, the profound seriousness. I ask a few introductory questions to which at first he gives only brief answers.

"Are your parents living?"

"No. They are dead."

"What work did they do in Cambodia?"

"My father was a doctor. My mother did housework."

"Would you also like to be a doctor someday?"

"No. I would like to be an airplane pilot." He tells me that once in 1974 he flew in an airplane from his village to Phnom Penh.

"Was it exciting?"

"It was wonderful." He smiles at last.

In fact, I had not needed to ask him if his parents were living. Neil gave me Ty Kim Seng's background earlier while we waited for the boy. Ty Kim Seng's father was shot to death by a Pol Pot firing squad, for no reason other than that he was a doctor. The policies of the Khmer Rouge included the execution of all Cambodian intellectuals. The definition of a Cambodian intellectual was quite flexible. It included dancers, artists, the readers of books. Under Pol Pot it was a capital offense to wear eyeglasses, which signified one might be able to read. At the age of five Ty Kim Seng watched his father being taken away in a helicopter. A few days later the body of his father was returned to his village, also by helicopter. For a long while in Khao I Dang, Ty Kim Seng only drew pictures of helicopters.

His mother died of starvation a few years later. By then, Ty Kim Seng belonged to the mobile work team and he no longer lived at home. His mother remained in their village, in which nearly everyone was starving. Much of the country was starving. Ty Kim Seng received word that his mother was very weak, and he managed to be taken to her. The night before she died he came to her bedside and saw how swollen she was, how weak her voice, with what difficulty she was breathing. The woman held her son's hand and told him that very soon now he was going to be an orphan, that he would have to be strong and look out for himself.

Then her eyes focused more clearly for a moment, and she said to her son: "Always remember your father's and mother's blood. It is calling out in revenge for you." She then told him to leave her room and to try to sleep.

At the time, Ty Kim Seng was keeping a diary, on which he would rely as a source of solace. He described this diary to Neil, but he had lost it by the time he came to Khao I Dang. In it he would begin his entries, "Dear Friend, I turn to you in my hour of sorrow and trouble." On the night his mother spoke to him he could not sleep, and he wrote in his diary how helpless and frightened he felt. In the morning his mother was dead. He knelt at her bed and he prayed. Then he walked to the house of a neighbor and asked that man to bury his mother beside his father in the village cemetery. Ty Kim Seng brought a shirt with him as payment for this service.

The neighbor and his wife carried Ty Kim Seng's mother in their arms to the burial ground, the boy walking several paces behind them. Ty Kim Seng was himself quite weak and thin. The neighbors buried his mother, burned incense and departed. Then the boy knelt by the grave and burned three incense sticks of his own. Finally, he took a handful of dirt from each of his parents' graves, poured it together in his hands, and beseeched his dead parents to look after him. Afterward, he returned to the mobile team.

"Do you feel your parents' spirit inside you now?"

"Yes, it talks to me. It tells me that I must gain knowledge and get a job." He says that knowledge makes people good.

"Does your spirit still tell you to take revenge?"

"Yes," solemnly.

"So, will you go back to Cambodia one day and fight the Khmer Rouge?"

"No. That is not what I mean by revenge. To me revenge means that I must make the most of my life."

I place before him one of the other pictures he drew when he arrived at Khao I Dang, one that Neil showed me before, along with the skeleton drawing. "What is happening here, Ty Kim Seng?"

The drawing is of three boys, stick figures, standing to the side of several gravestones at night. The background consists of a large mountain with a leering yellow moon resting on its peak. Perched on a tree is an oversized owl, whose song, says Ty Kim Seng, is mournful.

"One day I left my mobile team to go find food for myself, to look for yams. I was very hungry. I met two boys, and together we came upon a mass grave of thirty bodies. They were piled up and rotting. The Khmer Rouge soldiers found me. I lied and told them I had gone for firewood. But they punished me. They bound my hands to a bamboo stick behind my back. I was tied up without food for several days."

He is asked what it is that makes a man strong. He tells me, "a spirit." Is there a spirit within him? "Yes. I talk to my spirit. I tell my spirit that I must study diligently and work in order to find a home in America. Or perhaps in France." Yuom explains that France is much on Ty Kim Seng's mind these days, because he has recently learned that his older brother lives there. The boy hopes to join his brother in France eventually, though for the present that is unlikely. The refugee allotments for all countries are quite low now.

"Is the spirit that makes you strong that of your mother and father?"

"Yes. My spirit told me how to find my way to the border when I escaped from the mobile team." Neil told me that before making his way to Thailand, the boy walked more than sixty miles to Phnom Penh, hoping for news of his brother. I see him doing so as he talks, traveling mainly at night to avoid detection, the small face alert in the dark. I ask him if he believes his spirit will always guide him toward the right destinations. He says yes, definitely. "One day it will lead me home."

Presenting his drawing of the orange skeleton, I ask if he would explain it too. "I drew this after the death of my mother," he says softly. "I ate leaves then. That is why there is a tree in the picture."

"If you drew yourself today, would the picture be different?"

"Yes, very different." He looks happier. "Here I have food. And there would be a smile on my face."

"Would you do a self-portrait for me now?" Unhesitating, he moves to a long worktable under a window at the far end of the hut. An elder provides him with paper and crayons, and he works in silence. The noise of the other children has abated momentarily, the only sound being an occasional squawk of a late-rising rooster. Soon the boy returns and presents me with his drawing, which is not a self-portrait at all, but a bright blue airplane with green doors, green engines and a red nose and tail.

"But where are *you*, Ty Kim Seng?"

"I am the pilot!" He points himself out enthusiastically. "We are flying to France!"

Yuom brings a second child to the table. I am beginning to feel like a village official, a census taker. At the window beside me, a square hole in the wall, little faces pop up and down, vivid with curiosity. Nop Narith performs the *wai*. He is Ty Kim Seng's size and age, has shaggy black hair and great buck teeth that gleam in a smile. He holds his left arm below the table. Nop Narith had polio when he was younger, and the arm is withered. Both his parents are dead.

"When the soldiers came to my house, they took our whole family away. Me they took to a mobile team. I never saw my parents again. But I have a photograph of my father. My father was worried that I could not take care of myself. Yet I feel guarded by his spirit. I dreamed that I saw him, and he promised that his spirit would protect me. In the dream he told me to gain knowledge and to take revenge on his killers."

I ask him what is the happiest time he has known. The Lon Nol regime, he says, because that is when his family prospered. Lon Nol deposed Norodom Sihanouk and was himself overthrown by the Khmer Rouge. "We had air conditioning then." I ask what to him is the most important thing in the world. He answers, "Diamonds and gold."

"Which would you rather have, a peaceful time or diamonds and gold?"

"Peace is worth more than gold," he says.

"Your father's spirit told you to gain knowledge. Does knowledge lead to peace?" He says that it does. "Your father's spirit also told you to seek revenge against Pol Pot's soldiers. Is it your plan to do that?" Again he says yes.

"What do you mean by revenge?"

The boy responds at once: "Revenge is to make a bad man better than before."

Two more children come to talk with me, and they, like Ty Kim Seng and Nop Narith, define revenge either as self-improvement or as working to instill virtue in others. I wish to ask Neil about this. When I considered the subject of revenge in Athens, I only noted its absence in the children I had met up to that point. I was defining vengeance conventionally. It did not occur to me that the idea could ever be applied in such a way as to make it an instrument of beneficence or generosity. Was this something cultural, I wondered. Something derived from Khmer history or from Buddhist doctrine? The Theravada version of Buddhism practiced by the Khmer centers on the Four Noble Truths, which define wisdom as abjuring worldly desires. Perhaps so worldly a desire as revenge would be thought to impede salvation.

Or was it simply a matter of political caution not to indicate that there was anything violent in one's nature, lest prospective foster families be scared off? That seemed the least likely, because in each interview it was the children, not I, who raised the word "revenge." Had they wished to conceal their hatred, they would not have brought up the subject. Neil tells me that in counseling the children he has not focused particularly on the idea of revenge, but that the responses given me so far fit in perfectly with everything else he has seen in the children. "They are very gentle," he says, "especially when you consider what they've come through."

We stroll together around the camp. The air smells of hot mud, the humidity as thick as the atmosphere of an indoor swimming pool. Flies alight on my shirt and my neck, five or six at a time. I should feel more uncomfortable than I do, but the noisy gaiety of the camp keeps any sense of discomfort at a distance. The sun is veiled again. The sky hangs low, like a gray fishnet over the straw roofs. Suddenly it opens, and the two of us are soaked in a shower as dense as a wave. Just as suddenly the rain stops. In a minute or two we are dry again.

A small boy rushes up to show off his English. "OK! Bye-bye! OK!" He scoots back to his pals, who congratulate him.

I remark on the villagelike appearance of Khao I Dang. Boothby conjectures that some families have been here so long awaiting resettlement that the camp may naturally have assumed a traditional cast. The only blatant signs of modernity are the blue mushroom-shaped water towers, the laterite roads and the Rehabilitation Center, a larger hut than the Children's Center, where molds for artificial limbs lie stacked on shelves like loaves of white bread. The people mill about their wat. Their gardens are crowded with tomatoes, scallions, cloves, lemon grass and "Cambodian traditional"—marijuana. Squash wobbles on the latticework between the huts. A barefoot woman carries an armload of morning glories. Beside the roads grow needle flowers with pointed petals of burnished pink, and *mai-ya-rab,* a tiny fern, a weed really, that shrinks away at the human touch but after a while restores itself.

"Cambodia has always been peaceful," says Boothby. "In some ways it was the least likely country in the world to get entangled in killing and destruction."

"How do the children understand all this?" I ask him.

"What comes to mind is really not an adequate answer. How they understand it perhaps fits into their idea of fate, of karma. But they see fate as contradictory. Many of the people here regard Sihanouk as part of their national fate. Lon Nol too. Yet Pol Pot and the Vietnamese may also be part of their fate. They don't know what life they are meant to lead. All this is confusing, uprooting. Here are a people who have come from a rich and ancient tradition, a deep culture. For centuries that culture was calm and whole. Now their traditions are decimated. They struggle across a border. In other words, they are taken away from everything that had come together to make them who they are. Here they are held in a hostile country. Their freedoms are limited. All this has to have an effect on the ways they look at themselves, the world, the future."

"Yet the children seem to know what freedom is, nonetheless." I tell him of the West Bank students who also understood freedom without enjoying it themselves.

"It seems to be rooted somewhere in their past experiences," he says. "In those few moments when they felt free, when they could make real choices in their lives. Somehow that memory has not been stamped out of them. When people suffer as much as these children have, hope almost becomes a mechanism by which they survive. Perhaps it is in their worst hours that the thoughts of freedom are created. Part of their optimism may be tied to experience, then, and part of it to something that exists in all of us. It's just *there*."

We continue this discussion over lunch in Aranyaprathet, picking up Matthew before we head into the town. Matthew was easy to spot in Khao I Dang; one only had to follow the clamor to a circle of onlookers. At a sidewalk café in Aranya, as it is called for short, I hear the now familiar greeting, "Dr. Matthew!" The café's proprietor not only remembers my colleague; he has not forgotten his favorite dishes. Neil appears bowled over by this; Matthew takes it as a matter of course.

Neil continues to describe what he has observed in the children. It is not all kindness and tranquility. He tells us many children use the same wiles in the camp that they employed to survive in the jungle and elude Pol Pot. There are even stories of children denying the existence of their parents within the camp because they have heard that an unaccompanied child stands a greater chance of being claimed by another country. One boy was desolate because his friend suddenly left camp with a family with which he had been secretly ingratiating himself for months. A ten-year-old was so eager to emigrate that he found himself wandering around back at the Cambodian border. He had stowed away on a truck that, he had persuaded himself, was bound for America.

"They grow desperate," says Neil. "The elders convince them that the U.S. is another Angkor Wat."

I picture the peaked towers and the stone gods always shown in photographs of Angkor Wat, and I begin to grasp what Neil meant when he referred to Cambodia's "rich tradition." On the road that morning Socua had also talked of Angkor Wat, at length and reverently. It seemed odd that such a place should sustain itself as a national symbol, so distant was the world of Angkor, the crown of the Khmer Empire, from Cambodia's current ravishment. The era of Angkor's greatness certainly lasted long enough, from the beginning of the ninth century to almost the middle of the fifteenth, or more than three times the life of my own country. But Angkor was sacked by the Thais in 1431. Four long centuries it lay in the jungle, the city and the temple choked by the roots of trees, until the French naturalist Henri Mouhot stumbled on its ruins in 1860 and resurrected the sculptured city. All this was rather a long time for a village people to retain their affection for a Renaissance period that must have meant almost nothing to their rice-farming ancestors.

Yet Socua had suggested this was not so, that there was no forbidding chasm between the royal courts and the lives of the peasants. I later read an inscription from the reign of Jayavarman VII, described as the last great king of the empire: "The pain of their subjects, and not their own pain, is the sadness of Kings." A link between Angkor and the common people would be evident in the folk dance performance of the children which I would see that afternoon. When Angkor Wat was sacked, a troupe of nine hundred classical dancers was kidnapped by the Thais, but the art survived in villages, the stylized movements of the wrist and elbow kept alive through the practice and discipline of generations. Pol Pot did his best to kill that too, of course. Still, a classical Khmer dance troupe managed to escape Pol Pot, to regroup in Khao I Dang; and now it tours the world.

Perhaps the essential richness of Cambodian tradition lay in persistence and regeneration. The city of Angkor and its wat stood to the east of Aranyaprathet, where Neil, Matthew and I chatted on, at a shorter distance than that between Aranya and Bangkok. I could imagine it both now and as it must have looked during those four centuries of abandonment: sun-cracked, rain-battered, its stone burst apart by the reclaiming wilderness. Then it was recovered, then crushed again, the re-

141

current battle between civilization and wildness giving this country its basic rhythm. The moral wilderness wrought by Pol Pot added human savagery to natural devastation, but the desired effect was similar, to crush beauty in the world. If Angkor Wat remained beloved by the people, it was perhaps because the temple was the eye of the country, the jewel, the source of radiance that could outlast every jungle, every killer.

Neil speaks of the unrealistic expectations of the Cambodian refugees when they settle in the U.S. He is especially alert to the problems wrought by such expectations, his own road to Khao I Dang having begun in California in 1975, when he worked with Southeast Asian refugees. Later, he continued that same effort in Boston. For adults who have waited so long to be resettled and who then learn that Angkor Wat is not to be recovered in America, he says, "there is incredible depression and disorientation.

"Yet here, among the children, I have been so moved and impressed by how wonderfully they are doing. I'm amazed how loving, how compassionate they can be." He remarks that he was both heartened and interested to discover that the Western practice of encouraging people to talk openly about their troubles has paid off here. He refers to Ty Kim Seng in particular, and to Peov, whom I am to meet after lunch. "She is still tormented, bound up inside, but she is light-years ahead of where she started." Later, after speaking with Peov, I wonder in fact if it is all that beneficial to place every experience within the human context. Therapeutically, it works, of course. So in that sense the practice is worthwhile. Still, one sometimes feels there are certain things people do to one another that ought not to be accepted within the map of human possibility. Not being a psychologist, I wondered if it wasn't better all around to hold a few nightmares outside the pale.

Not for someone like Neil, clearly. Listening to him describe his work with the children, I realize I am admiring both an individual and a type. I have seen his kind elsewhere on the journey. Lyons in Belfast; Zion and Benyamini in Israel; people

142

who spend their lives with the troubled young and give them their hearts. A woman I met on the West Bank, though not a psychologist, was also of this breed. Sameeha Khalil runs the Society of Ina'sh El-Usra in El Bireh, a combination kindergarten, secondary school, museum, folklore institute, and a general haven for Palestinian children that she built up with her own dogged will in the aftermath of the Six-Day War. She was called Um Khalil by the children and staff, and she looked *um*—built low to the ground, unlikely to topple. She is about sixty. Her voice is made for speeches, her hair tied back to promote the clear, essential face. When I told her she reminded me of no one so much as Golda Meir, she shrieked and fumed. Yet her life was devoted to unteaching the hate in the children in her charge. "You want to show them that life is not all hardship. There is joy too."

Before taking this trip, I paid no attention whatever to such people. In my mind I cast them casually in a corner with clergymen, Salvation Army volunteers and others whom I counted among the world's nicest, blandest occupants. Now, a little late in life, I began to see that people like Boothby, Zion and Um Khalil are among the least passive creatures, that there is more fire in their decency than in most men's ardor. Watching Neil relate his amazement at the charity of the children, I see that I envy this fellow. I envy his temperament, his gallantry. Tomorrow Matthew and I will be on our way to another country collecting a story, and Neil will be at the kitchen table again in front of another child.

Nep Phem is waiting for me by the time we return to the Children's Center. He is eighteen, has large teary eyes, is said to be a gifted artist. We execute our *wai*s; I am getting good at this. Asked how he came to be interested in painting, he says that a spirit visited him and commanded him to paint. "The spirit taught me how to draw." Asked why he takes pleasure in painting, he says that art makes people happy. "It allows me to give something to someone, and it allows him to love me in return."

He has had good news today. Nep Phem long believed that both his parents had been murdered by Pol Pot. Now he has learned that his mother is alive in Phnom Penh. He smiles constantly as he relates this story. The most beautiful quality one can have, he says, is patience. The most important, honesty. The best thing one may achieve is liberty. "If Cambodia were free, it would be peaceful." And how is liberty won? "Through patience," he says. He seems quite satisfied with himself, as if he has just deciphered a code.

But he is both less comfortable and less coherent when I raise the subjects of war and evil. I ask if he thinks that war making arises naturally. He answers, "War makes people die."

"Do people learn war or is it inborn?"

"War must be born in you."

"Can the impulses for war and peace exist in the same person?"

He seems agitated. "No, they cannot stay together."

"Which wins out?"

"Peace will always beat war."

When I discussed this conflict with Ty Kim Seng, he gave the same general responses and like Nep Phem appeared troubled as he considered the problem.

A twelve-year-old girl, Meng Mom, approaches the table next. She is puffy-cheeked and very shy. She toys with her purple sleeve throughout our conversation and only smiles and looks straight at me when I mention that her gold circular earrings are becoming. No other subject I introduce elicits a response. She will not speak of her father, who is long missing, or of life under Pol Pot. She will not make small talk. Yuom tries his utmost to encourage her. Still, nothing. Then once again I bring up the problematical question: "Meng Mom, why do men make wars?"

Suddenly she blurts out, "There are a lot of bad men in the world."

"How does someone manage to remain good if so many men are bad?"

144

"Good must fight the bad."

"Can good and bad exist in the same person?"

"No. Not together. They are in separate places. The good must beat the bad." All this is said quite rapidly. Then she is silent again.

I begin to suspect that the intensity with which the children contemplate the idea of good and evil residing in the same person has some connection with their unorthodox views of revenge as charity. That morning one of the other children I spoke with, Gnem Thy Rak, a boy of sixteen, told of watching a Khmer Rouge soldier cut a man's throat in the jungle. When I asked what it is that makes someone do so dreadful a thing, he like the other children responded that some people are born with a good spirit inside them, some with a bad one, and that these two warring spirits cannot coexist in the same person. He added further that there are many more bad spirits than good ones in Cambodia these days. To the question, then, of how the good may ever prevail, he replied, "The good spirit must revenge the bad spirit," meaning, I gathered, that while good and evil are discrete qualities, it is still possible for virtue to triumph by exerting its influence on the corrupted spirit.

The idea is admirable but illogical. If the world is divided between the predetermined good and the predetermined wicked, then how would either be susceptible to change by the other? Would it not have been simpler for these children to allow that good and evil do exist in some proportions in everyone and that the problem of mastery is a continuous struggle? In order to answer that with a sure "yes," one would have to appreciate the depth and extent of the evil these children have witnessed and experienced. And clearly, some of the things perpetrated by the Pol Pot regime were so far beyond the imagination that the idea of a good spirit coexisting with that degree of evil must have seemed intolerable. Was it possible, then, that the children made their neat division of the spirits because they felt that no people who behaved like the Khmer Rouge could conceivably have any goodness in them?

Still, that would not account for the deep anxiety in their eyes and voices as they confronted this issue. What might explain it, however, was their knowledge that those who were carrying on the acts of murder and torture were neither strangers nor foreign invaders but were their own people, their neighbors, perhaps their relatives. This odd fact pertained in Northern Ireland and in the Middle East as well, but the depth and extent of destruction in those places was nothing like Cambodia. The term genocide has been used carelessly and indiscriminately since 1945, but what Pol Pot did was genocide, tens of thousands killed in a sweep. Some now call it "autogenocide." The killers and the victims were one people: the same skin, the same hands. How does one explain such a thing to the satisfaction of one's conscience except to contend that some people must be born with one spirit, and some with another? To believe otherwise would be to suggest that Ty Kim Seng's father had in himself the capacity to be his own executioner, that Ty Kim Seng and Nep Phem and Meng Mom had that same capacity. It was a terrible thing to concede.

Could their idea of revenge thus be a way of dealing with the fear of evil in themselves? If they could see how dangerous a good and gentle people can become, was it not possible that the only form of revenge to which they might be susceptible would be the reassertion of greater goodness and mercy? Revenge, conventionally defined, cannot be taken against oneself. If hate destroys the hater, it does so doubly when the enemy is within. "Revenge is to make a bad man better than before," said Nop Narith. What the children meant by revenge might be that revenge is a self-healing act, a purification into compassion and wisdom, as Buddhism itself prescribes. Revenge is to be taken against fate, against a whole world of incomprehensible evil. Living well, in a moral sense, is the best revenge. Logical or not, such a thought was at least a way of avoiding the essential nightmare that each of us is his own beast in the jungle.

Peov enters the hut. We perform our *wai*s, she holding her gaze to the dirt floor. She is scared to death. Yuom tries to put

146

her at ease, but she does not respond and only speaks in whispers. Peov is a heavy girl now and soft-featured, although like Ty Kim Seng she says that she "met with starvation" in Cambodia. We talk about a friend of hers to whom she gives food. She defines a friend as someone to whom one gives food and who provides food in return. There are long pauses between my questions and her answers. A car honks outside the hut. I ask her if she likes to draw. *"Bahn,"* she whispers. "Yes." Eventually, she says she would like to do embroidery for a living when she grows up. Yuom and I ask Peov to tell us more about her wishes, but she retreats again.

Hesitatingly, I produce the drawing of which the Geretys told me and which Neil gave me earlier. I ask Peov to explain it for me. She takes it in her hands and studies what she drew: three children gathering rice in a field. A Khmer Rouge soldier has a rifle trained on them, "to keep them working." Off to the left in the picture is the device. It looks like a wheel with a hollow hub and spokes leading out to the rim. Or perhaps it is a doughnut with lines on it. Three extra lines extend from the outer rim at the bottom, giving the thing the appearance of a crudely drawn insect. At the top there is yet another line sticking out at an angle to the right, the end of which is attached to a small ring.

"What is happening here, Peov?"

"This is a picture of the Pol Pot time." She hopes to change the subject.

"Who are these people?"

"They harvest the rice."

"And what is this [the circular device]?"

"This is something you put on the head."

"Who puts it on your head?"

"The Pol Pot soldiers."

"What is its purpose?"

"To kill."

"Do soldiers do the killing?"

No answer.

147

"Is it the soldiers who work the device?"

She will not respond to this question. Not now. But she has answered it before. After a year of silence she at last explained the device, if not fully, at least enough to allow a guess as to how it worked. The children harvesting rice include Peov. She is the largest of the three. Whenever a child refused to work, he was punished with the circular device. The soldiers would place it over the child's head. Three people would hold it steady by means of ropes (the three lines at the bottom). A fourth would grab hold of the ring at the end of the other rope (the line at the top). The device worked like a camera lens, the areas between the lines in the drawing being metal blades. When the rope with the ring was pulled, the lens would close, and the child would be decapitated. A portable guillotine.

But it wasn't the soldiers who worked the device. It was the children.

Outside, the rain splashes down, then stops suddenly as before, and everything is hot again. The children are excited; they are about to perform the folk dances that Socua has arranged. Some older boys are shooting baskets on a hard dirt court. They seem pleased when I join in for a few minutes. I block a shot. They laugh in surprise. They did not know defense was part of the game.

Behind the wat is a shack where the coffins are kept before cremation; and behind that, near a patch of sweet potatoes, the crematorium sits in a clearing under a shed, like a doll's chapel. There is no activity here today. But the wat itself is busy preparing for the final day of the Buddhist Lent. A monk in yellow sits cross-legged on a table, while children crouched in a circle burn incense. The smoke is supposed to fly to heaven in order to beckon their ancestors to descend and join them.

Teenagers are playing soccer in uniforms on a huge dirt field. Youngsters occupy the playground. A naked baby stands before a swing, perplexed as to how to work it. A few other children busy themselves in the arts hut, painting, or carving elaborate wooden musical instruments like the *take* and the *kail*, which are used to accompany the dancers.

But most of the children are in the theater tent now, the "Khao I Dang National Theater," milling about and chattering with expectation. Matthew and I sit beside Socua on a long wooden bench in the front. She tells us what we are about to see. Then the bright pink curtains part, showing a backdrop painting of Angkor Wat that extends the breadth of the stage. The xylophone plays the waterdrop music. The dancers enter. The boys strut, the girls cock their hands and heads and do not smile, as the rules of the dance require. They glow with color, their dark brown skins set off by the deep blues, reds and greens of their sarongs and sashes. They do four dances, starting with a hunting dance in which a small boy brandishes a spear and tries to look ferocious. The coconut dance is the most fun and the most intricate, as the children clap halves of coconuts from hand to hand. They flirt but do not touch.

The last dance is Ro Bam Kak Se Ko, the rice cultivation dance, presented in five parts. The first is the planting of seeds. The second is a dance of three scarecrows; the little ones in the audience howl at the masks. The third part is the cutting of the rice, and fourth is the tying. Finally comes the celebration of the harvest. The children prance joyously under a painting of a smiling moon. Over the loudspeaker an announcer explains: it was a good year.

S E V E N

Viet Nam

On the midnight flight from Bangkok to Hong Kong, I thought again of Ty Kim Seng, but not as he was in Khao I Dang. Rather I pictured the boy two years earlier, kneeling beside his mother, walking behind his two neighbors in the small, triangular funeral procession, later making his escape from tree to tree through the Cambodian jungle. It was the boy in the jungle I saw in my mind. I did not know a great deal about Khmer Rouge ideology, but I assumed that the jungle, as a state of primitive nature, was its ideal context. Whatever Pol Pot had in mind for children like Peov or Ty Kim Seng, in terms of Cambodia's future, had to be related to the purifying austerity of a life in the wild.

In their way, I suppose, the Khmer Rouge were followers of Rousseau, the last or the latest of the wild-eyed Romantics. If they believed that children ought to be reared out of the clutches of cities, they must have assumed with Rousseau that men are innately virtuous, that the children would realize their God-given worth within the state of nature the jungle provided;

151

this despite the fact that the state of nature was enforced by mobile slave-labor camps. That the Khmer Rouge ravaged their own country in order to achieve its purification must have struck them as necessary and honorable. Implicit in the slaughter of doctors and eyeglass wearers was the idea that all civilized society is corrupt, thus requiring the baptism of fire.

Yet it must have been clear to the children, indeed to anyone who had to deal with the Khmer Rouge, that the true corruption of civilization resided with the advocates of the antisocial, anti-intellectual life. All the ills that the civilized world displayed could not match the pure evil and barbarism of those who stuck bayonets into pregnant women, or who invented a guillotine for children and then forced them to use it. I remembered the *Wild Boy of Aveyron,* that remarkable story of a child, about the age of Ty Kim Seng, who lived as a savage in the forests of southern France before suddenly emerging one day at the end of the eighteenth century (he picked his time well) into the world of civilized men. Now there, surely, was Rousseau's noble savage, or so his observers anticipated. The trouble was the boy did not prove quite so noble. The many scientists who traced his moods and reactions found him selfish, gluttonous, raging; he showed no love or pity. In all respects the child performed as an animal. What his observers discovered, in fact, was a living refutation of Rousseau, that the perfectibility of the boy, however limited, was only indicated in a social state, and that all the virtues associated with being human were achieved in that state.

Would it not work the other way, I wondered. If one were to snatch a child from the civilized world, as did Pol Pot, and plunk him down among savages, would he not turn savage too? What seemed remarkable about Ty Kim Seng and the other Khmer children with whom I spoke these past days was that for a long time they had been exposed to a condition of life exactly opposite that of the wild boy of Aveyron, that is, to a state of uncivilization controlled by men. Yet they were not persuaded to join the barbarians. I began to suspect that Rousseau might be right about innate virtue after all, but not in the way he construed the idea. In Ty Kim Seng, indeed in all the Khmer children, I did see noble savages of a sort, children whose sense of charity and kindness seemed to grow out of nothing but themselves. If it was possible to take a certain number of these children and convert them to killers as the Khmer Rouge did, as the Nazis did with children before them, the fact is that the great majority were not susceptible to this conversion, and those who were, as Marie Gerety had pointed out, wound up close to catatonia, neither laughing nor crying.

The difference lay in the deliberate choices the children made, choices based on what they saw and on what they learned to value in the world. By the time I looked at the faces of Ty Kim Seng, Nop Narith and the others, I felt that I was seeing something astoundingly good, all right, yet the goodness emerged not from any state of nature, but from civilized society itself, from the best of what their families had taught and exemplified before Pol Pot descended on them, which lessons outlived Pol Pot and withstood his influence. Thus the charity of the children did not spring from inborn virtue but from the inborn ability to distinguish at quite an early age between good and evil, and then, being shown both, to choose good.

All along on this journey I resisted the idea that the children I was talking with were uniquely sanctified even though many of them sounded so, because I associated the idea of such sanctification with some harebrained, Romantic ideal, with the Rousseauistic ideal. I recalled the story of Coleridge strolling along an English country road and passing a mother and child, then suddenly yanking the baby from its pram and imploring it to tell him all about heaven, whence it had just arrived. After seeing the Khmer children, however, the whole process by which children of war acquired virtue seemed far simpler and more plausible. The fact is that children learn everything very quickly by observing adults. Why then should they not, by observing adults both civilized and savage, learn the wisdom of gentleness as well? In short, a child did not have to be born good any more than he had to be born knowing how to read. Yet just as he may yearn to read after a very brief time of staring blankly at books, so may he yearn to be fair, generous and understanding because he notes that such qualities, like reading, lead to advancement, peace of mind, control over fate and a minimum of chaos.

Ty Kim Seng was held prisoner in a jungle. So were all the children I had met so far. Belfast was a jungle. The Israelis and Palestinians had succeeded in creating self-sustaining jungles. Lebanon is itself a jungle. In each of these civilizations children like Paul Rowe, Hadara, Ahmed and Ty Kim Seng survived in part by learning the laws of the jungle, but also by preserving and following their own laws as well. In *Lord of the Flies,* William Golding makes a point of confronting the mad boy Simon with the Beast, evil, the beast in himself and in all the stranded boys. I believed now that the children I saw had undergone a similar confrontation and had come out of it with the knowledge that if they were to exist in the jungle, it would have to be as civilized men and women. In a way, they used their gentleness as a weapon, a defense against capitulating to the jungles about them.

But the point is that they did so not because of any inborn enlightenment but because they had figured out something rationally. They simply saw where hatred and killing led, and they took another road. If the goodness of the children seemed mystical (which to me at times it did), it was at least equally practical. Their virtue was part of a spiritual process, to be sure, but it was also grounded in experience, observation and common sense. That, one could accept. There might be a benign nature that oversaw this operation, that looked out for the children as they made their decision for gentleness and charity, but the decision itself, like an acquired trait, was merely a way of living in the world as it is.

Why this conclusion so comforted me I cannot say, except to acknowledge that I had been growing increasingly uneasy with the idea that I was observing a quality in the children akin to original innocence. What I now felt I was in fact seeing was neither original nor innocent, only the construction of wisdom based on experience. If this thought made sense, it allowed for the existence of the Khmer Rouge children and for the Nazi youth, for any of those who freely made different choices. Experience encourages other things than wisdom. The thought also allowed for the children I did not meet, but assumed were there—the cruel children, the bullies, the tormenters, the ones who soak cats in gasoline and set them ablaze, who tear the legs off frogs and terrify old people, who belittle newcomers, razz cripples, smash the prized possessions of others, destroy property, gang up, ridicule, find the sore spot and hammer home. Children are like that too, some of them. I grew up with kids so skilled at psychological torment, I shudder to imagine how they use their gifts as grown-ups. They were not children of war, of course, though they were born during a war; they were the children of the privileged. Still, I was sure that if I looked intently enough I would find their counterparts in the countries on my journey, if in smaller numbers.

Yet I was equally certain that just as the hateful children of my childhood constituted a tiny minority of the children I grew up with, so the children of war who acquired the trait of hatred were the exceptions that proved the rule. And the rule seemed firm. One lasts longer and lives better in a gentle state of mind; therefore, a gentle state of mind must be worth achieving.

If this were so, however, why did it not apply to children in all destructive and menacing circumstances—American slum kids, for instance? Why didn't they develop the same self-protecting techniques of compassion and mercy? They are children of war, God knows, skulking through their jungles, scavenging for lives. Like the children of Cambodia, those now growing up in Harlem, Watts, Roxbury, or for that matter in any of the world's abandoned wastes, are brutalized, orphaned, starved, deprived of companionship, friendship, love. They seem to offer little love in return, little charity.

The difference may have something to do with the suddenness of the assaults on children of fighting wars. Slum kids die slowly, over long generations, their lives eroded at so languid a pace that even they would have trouble tracing their disintegration. For the children I had met, death explodes like a car bomb or comes shrieking through the trees. They simply may not have time to cultivate their hatreds or to learn to accept the hatred of others as normal. Their exercise of charity may thus be an automatic reaction as well as a considered decision, a striking back with the opposite of what strikes them: generosity for cruelty, peace for war. When such a reaction works successfully against harm, it eventually becomes an established tenet of behavior and enters an unwritten code of laws, a survival kit.

Deep down I doubted whether such a process of thought and action can ever be anatomized the way I was attempting it. Of the Khmer children's capacity for hope, Neil Boothby concluded, "It's just *there*." In some ways I believed that was true of the children's capacity for gentleness as well. When, in *The Tempest,* Miranda steps out of her cave and gazes upon the only human beings she has ever seen, except for her father, the girl exclaims: "How many goodly creatures are there here! How beauteous mankind is! O brave new world, that has such people in't!" The fact is Miranda is looking at a gang of murderers, traitors and lechers, the very same crowd that tried to kill Miranda when she was a baby. Yet her untutored response to the sight of them is joy and wonder. The play is one of Shakespeare's last, a final judgment. If joy and wonder could be "just there" for Shakespeare, they could be so for me.

At least in part. Still, if I did not entirely believe that the children went about doggedly developing goodness in a mechanical process of self-protection, neither could I believe that everything was "just there" to begin with. I believed something of each. Perhaps what I was learning on this journey that now carried me to the far side of the world was that faith and reason were compatible in this matter, for I was unable to dwell in one region for very long without coming to the border of the other. This both pleased and tickled me. Perhaps I was going the old

Westerner's route, growing Oriental in the East, a Buddhist emerging like a lotus from the mud. I did not feel like a lotus. I felt quite simply that I was approaching a truth, and that I was doing so not by my labyrinthine ruminations but by following a straight path from country to country, child to child.

Now, by way of Hong Kong, I came to Viet Nam.

In Thailand it had seemed strange and removed talking with children outside their own country and away from their war. It would seem more so talking with the Vietnamese children in Hong Kong, not only because Hong Kong is a long way, in every sense, from Viet Nam, but because no war is being waged in Viet Nam these days, not a shooting war. For the first time in forty years the country knows a kind of peace. There are no gun battles, no shellings, no street riots in Viet Nam. One side has won, one side has lost. The losers have been given the choice of hunger, "re-education" or the sea. I would be meeting with children who chose the last, who crawled aboard boats that sailed a thousand miles up the South China Sea toward deliverance not from a war but from the consequences of war.

I wondered, in fact, if the Vietnamese children, while not in the thick of fighting at the moment, might have suffered more than the other children of war, at least in terms of variety. Like the Belfast children, they have known civil war; like the Khmer, terrorism and guerrilla war; like the children of Israel and Lebanon, they have seen bombing raids and artillery attacks; and their land, like that of the West Bank children, is now occupied. Beyond these, they have also experienced a personal, internal war over whether to leave their families and make an escape on their own. The children I would meet had to decide between home and freedom at a very young age, and having chosen in favor of freedom, or a chance of it, they imposed the most damaging effect of war on themselves. They opted for separation, for a loss of love.

At our hotel the first morning in Hong Kong, Le Ba Nhon, our interpreter, prepares us for what we will see. He has observed that a great many boat children, especially those whose parents were left behind in Viet Nam, seem deeply troubled and disturbed. "Some are wild, some are melancholy." Nhon is himself a boat person. His frame is slight, but strong, and he has dark, critical eyes opposed by an eager smile. A former middle-level civil servant in the Nationalist government, Nhon was imprisoned when the Viet Cong invaded the south. He made his escape to Hong Kong not quite a year ago. Doing so, he was forced to leave his young wife and their three-year-old son. He sends them money now by way of an underground mail service and hopes eventually to buy their freedom. Nhon recalls the day the Viet Cong took control of his office. "They did not sit on the furniture. They crouched on the bench tops like apes. It was then I realized we had lost to the apes."

We are at breakfast in the brand-new, indeed not quite finished Holiday Inn of Kowloon, the large, busy peninsula directly across the harbor from Hong Kong Island. Nhon has been introduced to us by Ross Munro, *Time*'s Hong Kong bureau chief and a China scholar, a man in his early forties with a square jaw and a rich voice. Ross has already endeared himself to Matthew and me by telling the German proprietors of the Holiday Inn when he made our reservations that I was editor-in-chief of Time Inc. and Matthew my right-hand man. Thus when we arrived from Bangkok at two in the morning, Matthew and I were greeted in the Valkyrian lobby by the entire hotel management, including the manager, all dressed in morning coats and bowing furiously. In contrast, Matthew and I were dressed in sweat-blotted shirts, and jeans and chinos respectively, having come directly to the Bangkok airport from Khao I Dang. I imagined this confirmed our high station to the Germans, since no one but the powerful would dare to look the way we looked.

So great was their respect for me particularly that I was given a suite of rooms on a floor at which elevators would not stop unless one used a special elevator key. Matthew's rank was not exalted enough for such a suite, which meant that as the week went on, if Matthew wanted to see me, he would have to phone first so that I would arrange for the elevator to stop at my floor. These circumstances, I told him, put the proper distance between us. On the night of our arrival, however, Matthew's room was not quite ready (the Germans apologized to their toes), and I agreed to share my quarters with Matthew for one night only. The hotel would appreciate that a man in my position could not be expected to sleep with the help. At this, Matthew adopted an obsequious stance and an Indian accent and stooped to pick up my bags, all of which baffled the Germans but seemed hilarious to us, at two in the morning.

The account of this nonsense delighted Nhon way beyond its worth. For all his evident and abundant geniality, Nhon clearly functioned under a great strain, which could be read in his face, and his work with the children in the refugee camps had not eased that strain. He was neither paid nor hired for that work; he took it on voluntarily. Being one of the elders in the camps, he saw that his fellow refugees, the children in particular, needed a source of guidance and solace. Nhon, who spent several years in the U.S., has a degree in mathematics from Columbia. A man of his experience and ability was of immeasurable use to his countrymen as a connective between their solitude and their suddenly adoptive world. In but a few months Nhon had picked up a smattering of Chinese in Hong Kong. Such feats, I soon learned, were typical of him.

He will first take Matthew and me to the refugee camp called Argyle 4, named for the street on which it is located. We should find some children there, he says. More will be scattered among the other camps. There are some fourteen thousand Vietnamese in Hong Kong now, down considerably from the seventy-four thousand that spilled into the city at the end of 1979. Still, it is a large number. At one point in 1979, the boat people were filling the camps at a rate of more than six hundred a day, some arriving on freighters that picked them up at sea, others by the small junks on which they embarked. In a few days I would see such an arrival firsthand: a crowd of stunned people, exhausted from a month on the open water, their faces a sea log of fear, courage and sorrow at having left behind, probably forever, everything they cared for.

By now, Ross tells us, the Hong Kong immigration people have the refugee situation pretty well under control. Once the boats dock, the refugees follow a set procedure. Unlike the Thais, the Hong Kong authorities do not consider these refugees illegal entrants and in effect have given them a status close to citizenship. For six days they will undergo health examinations, be given a chest X ray, and be checked for TB and malaria. Then they will live for a while in the Jubilee Reception Center, where all refugees must be processed before going off to any of four camps: Argyle 3 and 4, or Kai Tak East and North. Like the Jubilee Center, all are located on Kowloon Peninsula. In the camps, the children will go to school, kill time and wait for a sign from Europe, Australia or America.

In this respect, their situation parallels that of the Cambodian children at Khao I Dang, except that their hopes of resettlement are justifiably higher. But in temperament the Vietnamese children seem quite different from the Khmer. On the whole they are wilder and more independent, either because of their greater freedom in the camps or because of something characteristic. This difference is evident as soon as one arrives at Argyle 4. Argyle 4 used to be a storage depot for Hong Kong's armed forces. It feels odd to go there directly from the Holiday Inn, from the businessmen in pressed suits hailing each other in the lobby to the refugee camp in the middle of the same city. Yet Argyle 4 seems no refugee camp if Khao I Dang is one's standard. The place looks more like a teenage canteen, the kids loitering in clusters near the aluminum shacks like teenagers in any poor city neighborhood, their self-possession equally dopey and sinister.

"They hated the idea of school at first," says Pearl Chan. Pearl, at twenty-four, is the head teacher at Argyle 4. She learned her English in Saskatchewan and now instructs the Vietnamese in whatever they need, including English, handicrafts, physical education and how to adjust to the U.S.A. All adjustments are difficult. In Argyle 4 a gang of six welcomed Pearl on her first day of work with fistfuls of stones thrown through the classroom window. Many Vietnamese children in the refugee camps never went to school before, or quit very early. Many are country kids. Many were accustomed to running wild back home and have never conformed to an institution. In one class, Pearl tried to teach them to make birthday cards, but the children did not know what a birthday was. "They have no celebrations," she says.

"Yet some are catching on surprisingly well." A fine pencil drawing of a classroom shows open books resting on four desks in neat rows, with the teacher's desk elevated in the rear.

Generally, the art work of these students seems to have made the same progress as that of the Belfast, Israeli and Khmer children. The children start out doing pictures of bayonets and bombers; then, as their distance from danger lengthens, they graduate to faces and to houses in fields. One boy drew an elaborate marketplace, complete with shops and a clock tower, and he crayoned "Viet Nam" in red block letters over the entire scene. When given a free hand, the children usually draw Viet Nam in tranquillity. Pearl shows me a picture of a family at dinner, with mother, father and child seated formal and erect at a large round table covered with small dishes of food. But there is less serenity in the children themselves, in the older ones especially, she says. On the way in I saw two teenagers stripped to the waist, Indian wrestling on a high, arched roof.

Nhon has discovered Trung and Ha, who are brothers. We talk in one of the reception rooms. Trung appears fidgety, looks as if he is about to leap from his bench and hurl out the door. The boys are sixteen and fourteen respectively, and they are alone. Their father, a former officer in the South Vietnamese Army, was thrown into a "re-education" camp; their mother did not make it out of Viet Nam. Trung wears an oversize watch and a blue and white rugby shirt. He cracks his knuckles as he talks. Ha broods and talks less, but he voices his ambitions "to study hard and grow up and return to take revenge on the communists." Trung preaches love and compassion, yet asserts that revenge is the duty of all the Vietnamese people, and it is his own wish in particular. Unlike the Cambodian children, his definition of revenge is standard. Both boys would like to be doctors eventually, but when faced with a question similar to that posed to Ahmed in Lebanon—whether, as a doctor, he would treat a wounded communist as an enemy or a patient— Trung does not hesitate to say "enemy."

"But you are Buddhist," I remind him, "and Buddhism prohibits the taking of revenge."

"It is not against Buddhism to take back the happiness that belongs to you."

They both remember the war, in fragments. An explosion in the marketplace in Chuong Thien in 1972; a soldier running away; "in the morning I saw thirty-five VC corpses." Asked why he thinks men make war, Trung avoids the generality and cites the communists: "They were too poor and too savage, so they sought a fight." Do all men have the capacity to be savage? "No, only some." Does it feel good to hate the communists? "No. But it gives you a kind of strength."

"Trung," I ask, "if you should ever return to Viet Nam and settle down, would you want to have children there?"

"Yes. And I would always tell them to fight the communists."

"And you, Ha?"

The boy is silent for a moment, then turns to Nhon and speaks in a low twang, like a guitar being tuned. "I want no children," he says. "The world is an unhappy place for children."

Nhon tells me that the room in which we are sitting is sometimes used as a detention area for boys who get out of hand, stray from camp without permission, fight or otherwise cause trouble. Pham, the boy we are to speak with next, has a reputation as a troublemaker. He enters barefoot, in jeans and an undershirt, and positions himself directly under a modern ceiling fan that rotates like a searchlight as the blades spin around.

The ceiling is milk-white like the walls, like the tops of the benches. Someone has crayoned blue and pink lines on the floor. A crushed Coke can lies in a corner. Pham talks in long, sustained stretches, gulping for air as he goes.

He is seventeen now, and was eight and living in Hanoi during the December 1972 bombing, the American "Christmas bombing" of North Viet Nam. He remembers his family sitting around and talking together, "telling intimate things, sentimental things." Pham uses "sentimental" to mean tender, emotional. Then they heard the air raid warning on the radio. Other families ran down to the shelters, but Pham's father said it was not necessary for them to go anywhere. "If it is your fate to die, you die. If it is the family's fate to die, better to die together." They survived. Pham would not have obeyed had he not trusted his father's judgment. Like his father, Pham is headstrong, proud of his stubbornness. Of the communists he has no doubts: "The entire population wants to rise up against them. But there is no leadership, no organization. The whole country is a house in chains." Asked if he has the capacity to become such a leader, he replies he would need guidance but he feels he has the necessary courage.

Some of his courage has been shown already. At fourteen Pham wanted to join a national soccer team, so he left home, working his way up to a class B league by the time he turned sixteen. Then he returned to Hanoi, but the police came around to sign him up for the draft. "I did not want to become a soldier for the communists." Eventually, he left the country and his "sentimental life" behind, hiding aboard a junk that barely held ninety-three refugees and that suffered, among the standard hardships, a terrifying storm, and a doldrum in which Pham remembers sitting soaked to the skin as the boat spun in circles on the still sea. Yet he contends he was never afraid. "Life consists of difficult moments and of happy moments," he says. "In order to earn a happy time, you have to suffer hardship."

I ask, since he is an athlete, if he believes in rules. He says he does. I ask then if he has ever broken any rules. He answers without embarrassment that he has broken rules both in Viet Nam and here, that he has gotten into many fights. "In Hanoi I even beat up the police." There is no discernible swagger.

"Why did you break the rules?"

"Because they were against my conscience."

"Do you always decide, then, which rules to break and which to obey?"

"That's right. Everybody does."

"So were the North Vietnamese right to take over the country?"

"No," emphatically. He seems unconcerned that I am toying with his philosophy.

"But they were acting according to their consciences," I point out.

"Yes," he says, showing no sign of his imminent triumph. "But all consciences do not have the same value."

It is hard for me to tell if the relentless anticommunism expressed by those I have met so far is genuine or is geared to please Americans, with whom these children hope to live. Nhon tells me that from his viewpoint the hatred of the communists is sincere, but he cautions me that his own contempt for the Viet Cong is so deep and thorough, he may be blinded on the issue. He also points out that not all the refugee children are as willful as these three. Nhon introduces me to an eighteen-year-old boy named Vu who believes that "wars just happen." He left Saigon only out of obedience to his parents. There are others who are too confused and shaken to know what they think, swearing vengeance in one sentence, promising forgiveness in the next. Thanh, who is sixteen but could be any age for the wildness of his appearance, rails against war: "The big shots never want things to calm down!" It is known for a fact that Thanh was caught directly in the Christmas bombing, but when asked to describe the experience, he denies he was there. His eyes fill his bony face. His hands leap first to his long straight hair, then to the T-shirt with the palm tree on it. He shouts in a babble that he has never seen war.

"You have to remember," Nhon tells me later, "that war has been the only condition in Viet Nam since World War II. People do not think about war as if it were a sudden accident and therefore something that can be studied with perspective. There is no perspective. From 1944 on, you were fighting either the Japanese, the British, the French, the Americans or your own people. That is the history of Viet Nam. No Vietnamese, adult or child, sees war as distinct from history."

The following afternoon we take a look at Vietnamese history as it bobs and floats in Hong Kong Harbor. Ross has hired a boat for the day so that we may examine the abandoned junks and get a sense of the city as well. Beside Ross, Matthew, Nhon and myself, are Ross's wife Julie and Bing Wong, many years a *Time* correspondent in the Far East, whom I long wanted to meet from having seen his name on files in New York and thus conjured an image of a sprightly Chinese emperor. I was not far off. Bing Wong said almost nothing during our half-day tour, but his inner contentment controlled the company. As we pull out into Hong Kong Harbor, he takes a permanent post by the stern and stares calmly at the water as if he were entering an ancient dream.

"How much do you know about Hong Kong?" asks Ross. He is visibly pleased to learn that I know almost nothing, my ignorance giving him the occasion for delivering an enthusiastic lecture. I saw a similar eager look on the face of David Aikman, *Time*'s bureau chief in Jerusalem as he too, one night, looked down on the city that was his province and gave it shape for me. There seems this strong, strange attachment that foreign correspondents develop for the places they are assigned, as if the countries become their protectorates. Harsh criticism mixes fluidly with heaving waves of sentimental affection. Playing both native and outsider, they have the impossible task of spying on their own feelings. Yet they seem to pull it off. As I moved from region to region on the journey I sometimes wondered if the correspondents resented that I would swing in and out and soon be headed home. Then I realized that for them these distant outposts were home, that in their eyes it was I who had no fixed position.

What little I did know of Hong Kong lay in a jumble of history-book facts: the British seizure of the islands in the mid-nineteenth century; the Opium Wars; the so-called New Territories that are supposed to revert to China under the terms of a ninety-nine-year lease wrested by the British from a shaky Chinese dynasty in 1898. The latter is the topic of Hong Kong parlor discussions, talk that will grow more frantic as the year 1997 approaches. The specter is that of the Chinese hordes reclaiming Hong Kong and converting the city from humming capitalism to brooding communism. Ross says this is unlikely, that a new lease will probably be drawn up. The principals will find some way to keep Hong Kong as it is. "It is too important for business. Everyone needs Hong Kong."

We chug through the water, heading for the area where the Vietnamese boats are kept but taking our time. Ross names the bays around us: Deep Water, Repulse, Stanley, Big Wave. "The harbor is the city," he says. He lists the people who have sailed here to settle: Chinese, Eurasians, British, Portuguese, Germans, Jews, Indians. "Five and a half million by official count, but you can probably double that number." I look back at Hong Kong Island, at the silver-block office buildings piled at the base of Victoria Peak. Manhattan compressed against the Rockies. I think, Money. Ross confirms this.

The picture he paints is of the freest enterprise: the steepest rents, the swiftest fortunes made and lost, coins jingling down chutes; of more getting and spending on these few overcrowded acres than any place else on earth. "To Victoria and Albert, the Treaty of Nanking was a royal joke. Who needed Hong Kong? Now look at it."

We survey the boats lying at anchor. Cargo ships from Panama; yachts from the Philippines; junks; a three-masted schooner, white in every part. In an inlet a row of pleasure boats squarely faces a crowd of sampans, like rich girls lined up in front of poor boys at a charity dance. Ross and Julie talk admiringly of the oldest boat people of Hong Kong, the Tanka and the Hoklo, who have dwelt for centuries on the waters off southern China, never leaving their boats, fishing and sleeping on their boats, having babies in the holds. We come upon an old woman in a Tanka hat, an inverted wicker vase, poling her sampan silently alongside us. Her face is as wrinkled as a plowed field.

Gulls glide and swoop over the black satin water, their tummies hovering inches above the darkness. We cruise under a bridge, then through a channel. Ross points out our destination, Gin Drinker's Bay. This is where the boats from Viet Nam are stored and where they must be destroyed. For health reasons the Hong Kong authorities have deemed that the vessels be burned as soon as possible after arrival. The sun is fierce now, a vast white patch. As we drift into the bay, I see a hill of gray gravestones on our right and next to that a bright blue columbarium. To our left, on a rise of land, boats lie piled like skeletons. Nhon notices there are but a few boats now. There were hundreds when he was last here, including his own, the one on which he made his escape. A junk from Haiphong is marked with the number 1540. The boats are numbered sequentially as they come in. "Mine was 1418," says Nhon. He calls the bay an elephants' graveyard.

A junk that looks quite small to me, about thirty meters long, Nhon identifies as one of the larger vessels to make the journey. Such a craft would have carried three hundred people, he says, stuck to the timbers like flies. I spot several smaller junks, six meters long, that would have held ten or eleven. Two boys I would meet tomorrow escaped on boats this size. When they described the terror of their voyages to me, I envisaged the boats in the bay. There is no terror in this scene now, only a quiet sinking of the heart. The boats smolder. The engines, which do not burn, lie heaped like brown skulls beside the remains of a tiller that was forged with welded pipes. A dog scavenges in the ruins.

One junk remains intact, not yet hauled ashore for burning. I climb aboard and peer into the hold where people once huddled, a place ordinarily used to store a day's catch. Every timber is rotted. Nhon, who does not choose to explore with me, observes that the only area on these boats where passengers did not cling was near the engine, fearing suffocation from the fumes. The boat is typical, he says. It would have carried eighty. The life has gone out of his voice for a moment. I suddenly realize that he is not only grieving for the loss of his family or recollecting the difficulty of his escape. He is mourning Viet Nam. For Nhon, for the children I met yesterday and those I was yet to meet, for the tens of thousands who sailed, dazed, into Hong Kong Harbor the past three years, all that is left of Viet Nam are these boats.

Hooking out of Gin Drinker's Bay, we tour the rest of the harbor, purring softly in the heat past inlets and islands. Over there, rising into haze, lies China, the great nation of mystery for my Cold War generation. Someone mentions Macao. China and Macao. I should be more stirred than I am by these names, my mind prodded to wander. Instead, I remain anchored in Hong Kong. It seems the entire world to me, past and forever, a place where all the world convenes, and to which it sends representatives, like the boats and the refugees. Perhaps the world will end in Hong Kong. Perhaps its lease, like Hong Kong's, will be up in 1997, and all the frantic trading will stop on a dime. Sun thoughts. In the distance the sunlight ricochets off a McDonald's arch crowning an office building. Private houses cling to the sides of Victoria Peak. The higher you go, the richer you must be. I picture the junks stuffed with people, their segmented sails open like insect wings, gliding into the harbor under the bright tutelage of the houses.

Farther out we go until the islands we pass are the uninhabited ones, and no other boats are in sight. Suddenly we come upon an enormous gray structure, a huge rectangular steel box

Ty Kim Seng, whose father was executed and whose mother starved to death under the Khmer Rouge.

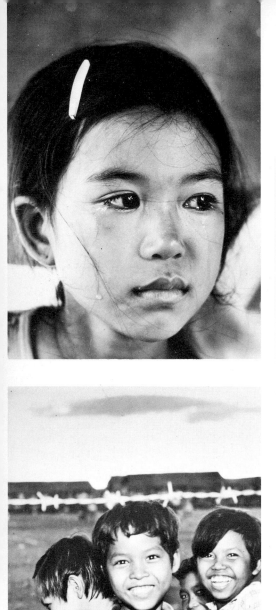

*Trinh, a Vietnamese refugee,
on the morning of her arrival,
crying for her father
who remained in Viet Nam.*

Vietnamese boat children arrive in Hong K

*Watching a soccer match
through a barbed wire fence
at Khao I Dang.*

*A small Cambodian in a
contemplative stance at the
Khao I Dang refugee camp
in eastern Thailand.*

bor after a month-long voyage from Haiphong.

*Two at the window
of a Vietnamese refugee
camp in Hong Kong,
waiting for a new country.*

Photographs by Matthew Naythons

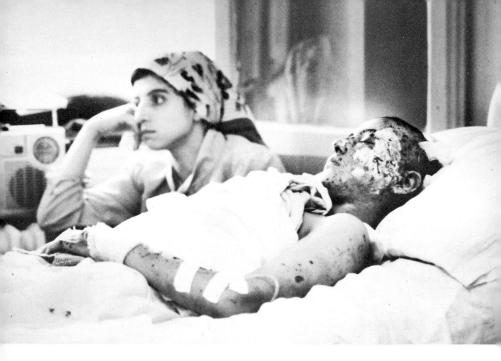

A teenage Lebanese girl, lying in the hospital, brain-damaged, after her house was shelled by Israelis in the summer of 1982.

Ahmed, a PLO soldier at the age of sixteen, manning a position near the airport in West Beirut July 1982.

Photographs by Bill Pierc

looming out of the water at a great height. It cannot be a boat. It seems five times the size of the largest aircraft carrier. Besides, it shows no smokestacks, no portholes or rigging, and it is not shaped like any boat. A dry dock perhaps, but surely the world's biggest. The name painted on its side appears to be Tarfax. Tarfax. Is Tarfax a company? Where is it located? What does Tarfax make? What does this structure do? We circle it like a minnow around a leviathan. We want to make inquiries, but there is nobody to call to, not one person visible anywhere on the immense hulk. Matthew jokes about a nuclear device. Ross suggests the Trojan horse. We circle again, and yet once more, picking up not a clue. Defeated, we retreat finally and head away, each of us glancing back occasionally at Tarfax, whose size does not seem to diminish as we recede.

"Pictures, anyone?" Matthew shows our pilot how to work his camera, and we pose. Ross, Julie, Matthew, Nhon and I stand with our arms about each other, grinning in the dying light. Bing Wong agrees to join us for one shot only. The clouds go dark, so thick that the sky seems streaked upon them, the sun a dab of orange floating down. Soon everyone grows quiet and apart, content to drift. Bing Wong resumes his position by the water. Nhon is seated at his side.

I assume that this is the last I will see of Hong Kong Harbor, but in two days, on a clear blue Sunday morning, Nhon, Matthew and I will be out here again, on a pontoon in the Western Quarantine Area, speaking to the newly arrived boat people with whom this story began. The girl Trinh will gape at Victoria Peak, I will compliment her on her yellow barrette, she will cry for her missing father. Nhon will cry, Matthew will cry and so will I. The first phase of my journey will be over. It's odd to think that at this moment, as we rumble back to port, how little Nhon, Matthew and I know of each other, and how, in the presence of Trinh we will know much more, though nothing explicit. Odd to realize too that at this point I believe I have seen it all, that I have covered the territory. I am wrong about that as well.

Tomorrow I will meet more Vietnamese children, at the camp called Jubilee, but I do not imagine their responses will differ from the Vietnamese I have met so far: a mixture of wildness, strong-headedness and anger. They seem less disciplined versions of the Palestinian children. Like them they sound loving and gentle when not focusing on their particular enemy. But they are confusing, nonetheless, not part of the patterns I found elsewhere. If they are less forgiving than the Irish or the Cambodian children, it may be a matter of national temperament. If they appear less generous than the Israelis, it may be because unlike the Israelis, they are not children of the victors. The ruling quality of those I interviewed so far seemed not aggressiveness, but frustration at their inability to win anything. Thus they flailed about much more than the Khmer children in spite of being generally more sophisticated and more familiar with the modern world. In some ways this flailing seemed superficial to me, a ceremonial rattling of arms, but I could not prove that in so brief a visit. I concluded that in the Vietnamese children one finds a little of everything that happens to children of war, that just as their country has endured all types of warfare for generations, so the children have come away from that variety made up of everything war can provide.

Looking out on the water, then, but not seeing it, I begin to write my story in my mind. I have my theme and my exceptions. I feel the structure start to close now, the way journalists often do, the hitherto shapeless experience finally finding or imagining its form, like a huge, heavy door shutting on a house that is not yet erected. Had I known that in twenty-four hours a boy named Khu would require me to reopen that door, I could have saved myself the effort.

In the morning, Nhon takes Matthew and me to the Jubilee Center, where we spend the first few hours talking with the supervisor and wandering among the refugee families. Nhon goes off on his own to find a couple of boys whose stories, he says, will interest us. Matthew and I patrol the camp, which is large but compact. It sits on approximately two acres of land at the

170

edge of Kowloon, directly across from Hong Kong Island, which we can see clearly. Fifteen hundred refugees live here now, in twenty-four four-story blocks. Filled to capacity, the center can hold up to sixty-five hundred. It abuts a fish-processing plant. I watch a girl and boy scoop for eels that have escaped from the plant into the sewers. The air smells of fish and the sea, the harbor lending vitality to the atmosphere which, one suspects, would be languid and seamy if the center were located inland.

The name helps too but only a little. The Jubilee Center was first built in 1935, the silver jubilee year of George V, for which the center was most likely named. Like Argyle 3, Jubilee served as a Japanese POW camp from 1941 to 1945 for British and Chinese soldiers. After the war, the Sham Shui Po Camp, of which Jubilee was a part, reverted to its original function as a British army barracks. It became a refugee center in February 1979 and since December 1980 has been administered by the Hong Kong prison department, whose clipped-voiced officers inadvertently give the place the feel of a prison. A door is marked "Superintendent Detention Camp." Windows are barred. The air is soaked with antiseptic. At the water's edge stands a high chain link fence, its upper portion bent outward at an angle to prevent entrance or escape.

Nhon introduces me to Tranh Van Be, one of the two boys he set out to find. We sit in a classroom in the basement of the building where the administration offices are located. The room is small, the size of a seminar room in a university. Two rectangular windows located high on one of the walls offer the only sources of air and light. The ceiling is whitewashed; the paint streaks down in cream-colored icicles on the maroon-brown walls. Upstairs, doors slam open and shut, and the ceiling of the classroom shakes with the hard stepping of the officers' shoes. Outside there is a steady, rapid hammering and the grating buzz of an electric drill driving into metal. Nhon explains that they are expanding the facility. He signals Be to sit beside

171

him on a white-topped bench. I face the boy from an old wooden desk chair.

"At Jubilee they call Be 'Buddha,'" Nhon begins. "You can see why." The boy looks up with a happy, vacant smile. His nose is flat, his face apple round, his ears stick out like china sea shells. He wears a purple T-shirt and yellow shorts.

"Would you wish to be like Buddha too?" I ask him.

"Yes," he says with a strange eagerness.

"Then you hope to be a man of peace?"

"No," with the same expression. This is the way our conversation will go.

He tells me of his adventures with the boat, how he made his escape from Saigon and how he fared on the voyage. Almost nothing is coherent. His father was a fisherman who sold shrimp heads for fertilizer. "One night two men came to the boat."

"To your father's boat?"

"No. I saw two men approach another boat and tell the boat master that they wanted to make a voyage, to leave Viet Nam. But the boat master said no, so they killed him. Then we all went out to sea, but we only had five kilos of rice, and there were fifteen men on board."

I ask Be to slow up. I tell him this is hard to follow. Did he actually see the boat master killed? Yes. One night he and his father were sleeping on top of the cabin on their own boat, when they overheard the two "masterminds" plotting to murder the boat master. "If you stab him here and here," said one to the other, "it will be enough to kill him." The boy indicates two points on his neck and stomach. Soon afterward, he heard the boat master groaning in the hold. When Be went below, he saw a young man sticking a knife in the boat master's bowels. "But this young man was also killed."

"On the boat?"

"No. On the island."

So he continues, first leaping ahead, then backtracking and contradicting himself. I ask him to recapitulate, and now he

172

says he neither heard nor saw the boat master being killed. I ask about the young man on the island, and he says that the island is where his father died. "It was a small island, perhaps fifteen meters across. There was a rock on it, and a tall light-house." A lighthouse in the South China Sea? I look to Nhon for clarification, but he too appears confused. The boy is speaking quite rapidly now, the leaping rhythms of his Vietnamese sounding like a European police horn. Suddenly he corrects himself again. It was not the boat master but his son whom Be saw murdered. No, that's not right; the boat master's son was killed at sea.

"What happened to your father, Be?"

"He died of hunger and was buried at sea." He pauses briefly, then looks back at Nhon. "No. He was buried on the island." Then his father was not buried at all but rather was left on the island to perish. "He just sat down beside a big boulder to die. And they left him there."

"Were you very frightened then?"

"No. We were so hungry, we all thought we were going to die. So no one was afraid anymore."

I try to steer him away from his story toward other topics, but without success. He has no thoughts about the morality of war. He has no opinion of himself. "I will know such things when I grow up." Does he hope to have children of his own some day? "No. They would make my life hard. They would urinate and defecate." I assume that Nhon is translating formally. The boy is speaking faster than ever. Yet his face remains cheerful. I ask only a few more questions: What is his happiest memory and what is his saddest? He responds that he has never seen anything happy or sad.

"Was not your father's death a great sadness?"

"No." Be smiles wanly. "Only my present loneliness makes me sad."

Seeing Be's frenzy, I begin to understand that the voyages of escape from Viet Nam constituted wars in themselves. "Even my voyage was terrifying," says Nhon. "And we were at sea

173

only thirty-nine days. Many voyages took much longer. They ran out of food early on. You hear talk of cannibalism." I picture the progress of the voyages clearly for the first time, working my mind back from the smoldering hulls in Gin Drinker's Bay to the moment when people like Pham or Be and his father first crept aboard small fishing junks and set out for a thousand miles of ocean. For a month or more these boats became island nations gliding through a truncated history. The people who started out full of hope soon grew fearful and suspicious. The cooperative became selfish, the healthy sick, the sick dead. Some of the passengers grew dangerous as the voyage lengthened. Some were dangerous to begin with. Locked in among them were the children, sitting body to body with adults in a stoic silence, watching for a change of weather or a change of mood.

"In a way, the voyages constituted our latest war," says Nhon. He leaves me to find Khu, the other boy he has been seeking. I gaze absentmindedly at the wire mesh on the classroom windows and wonder how it feels to be starving at sea. I muse on the subject of cannibalism. Last night I contended there are things one could not eat under any circumstances, but I knew this was not true. We were dining in an elegant restaurant, Matthew, Ross, Julie and I. Matthew and Ross got to talking about restaurants in China where there are holes in the centers of the tables. These are for the heads of the monkeys. The animal, they said, is stunned but not killed, and placed below the table top with his head propped up through the hole and his feet resting on a bed of burning coals. The heat from the red coals forces the blood to rise to the monkey's brain. The head is then sawed open before the customers and the brain spooned out, as if from a bowl.

Between the ensuing predictable jokes I questioned if I could ever eat such a thing, even under threat of starvation. Surely I could. People will do anything to live. People, as I have been reminded on this journey, will do anything.

So lost am I in this reverie I do not notice Khu until he is about to take his seat before me. For a moment I think it is my oldest child, Carl. There is no real physical resemblance, except that both boys are built strongly, with muscular legs, and both are fifteen. Khu is not as tall as Carl, though of average height for a Vietnamese fifteen-year-old, about five feet two inches. His hair, cut short, sticks up straight like a washed kitten's. There is a shaved spot near the forehead where two parallel gashes glow like a reddened equal-sign. The wound is part of his story. Khu's face is mouth-open flat, without expression. His eyes are so brown as to appear black. They cannot be said to show expression either. They seem their own depth, the vessels of what they have seen. It is for what they have seen that Nhon has brought Khu to me.

A shadow is lingering in the doorway. Nhon introduces Phuoc, a thinner boy with a narrow face who explains that he has accompanied Khu as his friend. Khu accepts Phuoc's presence without a sign of protest, but when Phuoc leaves the classroom a few minutes later and Khu is asked if Phuoc is indeed his friend, there is no qualification in his "No." Nhon suspects that Phuoc may wish to be Khu's friend now, but he was on the wrong side during the incident at sea. When the boys landed, in fact, they squared off for a fight, and for weeks they hurled challenges at each other. They may reconcile eventually, but Khu, who has a tendency to forgive, has a way to go before forgetting what happened in the boat.

Climbing aboard was easy. Khu, who was fishing by himself on a dock one day, simply saw the junk take off from Haiphong, and on he hopped. He did not say good-bye to his three sisters and brother-in-law, and there was no one else to consult, Khu's mother having died in 1976 of something in the stomach that "pricks and hurts," his father having died of a stroke two years later. Both parents were fishmongers, and Khu knows boats. The one he boarded was thirteen meters long. They were fifty-two days at sea. There were eleven voyagers to begin with. They had twenty kilos of rice on board and forty liters of water. When both gave out they used their fishing nets, and that was when the trouble started. A few men, "taking advantage of the others," fished for themselves at night. The boat master fought with them. Four people "fell" overboard. Seven remained.

The story is interrupted by the sounds of more sawing and drilling where they are expanding the center and by a metallic female voice issuing instructions over a loudspeaker at frequent intervals. Khu must be asked to let the noise abate. He would speak straight through it.

"Why were you hit on the head?"

"The boat master wanted to eat me." The tone is matter-of-fact.

"How do you know this?"

"The boat master told a boy who was a neighbor of mine to take a hammer and hit me on the head, so that they might eat my flesh. The boy told me." All this, I learn later, was verified, somewhat reluctantly, by the other voyagers.

"Why did you believe him?" I ask. "Did you see such a thing before?"

"No. But earlier in the voyage the boat master wanted to kill someone else for the same purpose. The man was so scared, he committed suicide. He struck the boat master on the head with a wooden bar and then leaped overboard." That left six.

"And how did they try to kill you?"

"They put a shirt over my head, and they hit me with something hard. I felt the men coming over to lift off the shirt. But I was still conscious. I heard the boat master order another man to cut my throat." I know I am staring too intently, but he does not seem to mind.

"At the moment they took the shirt off my head, they saw that I was conscious and that tears were on my face. I did not know what they were thinking. Then someone said, 'Khu, do you want to live?' And I said, 'Yes, of course I want to live.' So they untied me and took me into the cabin."

I see the sequence as if I were present in the boat: the selection of the uninteresting, solitary boy; the logic of it; the low-

176

whispered plotting; the appointment of the assassin; the blow; the raising of the shirt and the surprise. But then what? What, in fact, were those men thinking that held them back from murder? Mere pity? Or was it the recognition of Khu's tears as their own, the knowledge that the boy was not weeping to save his own skin, but theirs, that he was weeping for all those who did ever, or will ever, or do now devour their young? Jubilee is suddenly noiseless. No sawing and drilling. No amplified announcements. The sun is frozen in the lowest pane of the classroom window.

"What did you think when you realized that they were going to let you live?"

"I only thought I would die eventually, because the next day the boy who used the hammer on me was himself found dead. After the body was discovered, the boat master pulled it out of the hold. Then he cut up the body. Everyone was issued a piece of meat about two fingers wide." He indicates the size on his hands.

Khu was told to eat for strength, and he did. But he remembers thinking that if the people on the boat ran out of food again, he planned to jump overboard. He tells us he is afraid of the boat master still. Thanks to Khu's testimony, the boat master was jailed by the Hong Kong police. Khu is terrified that the man will be released and come after him.

For his part, he feels no hatred for the boat master whatever, only disapproval. He understood the necessity of eating the dead boy, and he observes that the fear of starvation may have driven the boat master to behave with unnatural cruelty. Unlike the Cambodian children, Khu acknowledges that there is the capacity for good and evil in everyone.

"Then would you kill a child in order to survive?"

"No," he says. He adds something else, but his voice is drowned out by a jet overhead. I lean forward and ask him to repeat himself, which he does, but too soon; the jet still obliterates his voice. He waits then, thinking I have understood him. I wait for the plane to pass, sitting in the classroom where the

177

teacher ought to be, looking blankly at the boy who looks at me. Sure of the moment at last, I ask him yet again to tell me what he said. He hesitates, confused.

"About the child," I tell him. "Would you yourself kill a child in that situation?"

"No." He repeats the words I did not hear, perhaps wondering if he has been unclear: "We go together in one boat. If we die, we die. I would not kill in order to live."

The window shows the sky deep blue; the sun must be nearly down. The boy remains hunched forward, waiting for more questions, but I have none. Almost as a social gesture I ask about his pastimes. He watches TV or plays table tennis. "I am only a beginner." His future? He thinks it limited. He quit school in the second grade, after his mother died. When he was at home living with his sisters and brother-in-law, he used to watch them repair boat engines, and he says it might be nice to do that work some day. Then he considers for a moment and decides that car engines would be even better. "Yes. I could work as an apprentice in a small shop." Does he have any friends in Jubilee? One, a man who occupies the bunk next to his. Khu has trouble falling asleep at night, so this man, who reminds Khu of an uncle, tells him stories. Khu favors one in particular: a fable of a coconut that turns into a person and falls in love. Khu knows his friend tells him these stories to help him sleep, but Khu always gets interested and stays awake to the end. I suggest we go upstairs for air.

Would Khu play table tennis with me? He seems eager for this and smiles for the first time in an hour. We wait our turn, standing beside the table which is located outside the building, under an eave on the harbor side. The two boys who are playing do not keep score; they only rally. When they notice we are waiting for the table, they relinquish it readily, appearing as content to watch Khu and me play as to play themselves. We too only rally. Khu's forehand is weak, but his backhand is quite good. We can keep the ball bouncing between us for ten shots or more. I watch his face intent on play. Nhon has left us for a moment; no interpreter is required here. We work up a sweat and then retire to stand together by the chain link fence, peering at Hong Kong Island and the night.

Now Nhon rejoins us, taking a position on the other side of Khu, who gazes at the island steadily.

"What do you think about when you look at Hong Kong?" I ask him.

"I see lots of lights which are beautiful. And boats."

"What do you think when you see all the boats?"

"The boats have lights too, which are also beautiful."

"What else is beautiful, Khu?"

The boy answers quietly, "Everything is beautiful."

Epilogue

Into the Fire

My first weeks back in New York, I found it hard to talk to anybody except my family and one or two friends. Even with them my conversation would start out spirited enough but soon would sputter and die entirely shortly thereafter. I spent much time either alone or studying the slides taken by Pierce, Adams and Naythons on the trip. Ostensibly, this was done for the benefit of the story on the children I was preparing to write, but in fact my picture gazing became a kind of ritual of preservation. I simply wanted to hold onto everything I had seen and heard, to prevent it all from splintering into the normal sights and noises of my life and merging with the traffic outside the Time and Life Building on the Avenue of the Americas. Gradually, I slid back to my routines, but not before fighting them off as long as possible, the way one sometimes sees a crazy old man, about to be dispossessed, board up his door and prop a shotgun in the window.

In the months that followed, I had both happy and unhappy news of the children. In April a Houston architect, Dave God-

183

bey, wrote to tell me that his family (photo included) had been corresponding with Paul Rowe since my story appeared, and that Paul was going to spend part of the summer with the Godbeys. At the end of July Dave wrote again, including a letter from Paul and another photograph showing Dave, Paul and Dave's teenage son Patrick smiling in bright sunshine and dressed to the nines. Paul wrote that on the first Sunday of his visit the Godbeys proposed to take him to the local Catholic church, but Paul opted for the Godbeys' church instead: "It really isn't very different." The thrust of the letter was to convey the wonder of the "Malibu Grand Prix" go-carts to which Paul had just been introduced. In the picture he looks both blonder and older than he did in Belfast.

Of Ty Kim Seng there came first a report that while he was attempting to rejoin his brother in France, his brother had returned to fight in Cambodia, and he was killed there. Then one day a letter arrived from a Quaker woman in Northampton, Massachusetts. Ty Kim Seng was living there with a foster family. The letter described the boy's introduction to the community, Ty Kim Seng being asked to stand before the congregation at a Quaker meeting so that all might look on him. I pictured him beheld by the New Englanders, the scene of mutual appraisal. Peov too was said to have found a foster home in New England, but I was not told where.

As for Khu, Nhon wrote me in January that both Khu and Phuoc had been rejected by the U.S. Department of Immigration for reasons unspecified or unknown to Nhon. One day, wrote Nhon, Khu approached him, "put his mouth close to my ear, and whispered: 'Arrange for me to go to Australia, please. I like Australia.'" Nhon doubts that Khu knows where Australia is. The incoherent Be also remains in the camps, but the brothers Trung and Ha are off to Holland. In May, Nhon himself made it out of Hong Kong and is now teaching Vietnamese in the U.S. Army Language School in Monterey, California, while mastering computers on the side. He sends whatever money he is able to save home to his wife and little boy, hoping

184

to buy an exit visa with a sizable bribe. Nhon's abiding fear is that his wife will panic and try to escape by boat on her own.

By June of 1982, then, the events that had occupied my thoughts so intently and compactly the previous nine months began to slacken like loosely coupled railroad cars. I continued to correspond with people I met on the journey, sharing news and memories, each communication growing briefer, cuter and more formalistic. This was as inevitable as it was dispiriting. For all the suffering I encountered during my five weeks around the world, for all the loss and waste, I had never felt more alive and purposeful. I missed my journey, selfishly, with all my heart.

So I am ashamed to admit that when the Israelis invaded Lebanon in June 1982 and announced that they were headed for Beirut, I was only partly dismayed. I worried for the safety of Ahmed, Lara, the baby Palestine, Samer and the other children I had met in Lebanon the previous September. From my self-interested point of view, however, the invasion presented two opportunities: to test the thesis of my original story and to witness a shooting war. The latter made me nervous, but it also provided a framework for the former that seemed absolutely necessary. In my story I had contended that the children growing up in the world's war zones are, by and large, loving and gentle. Now Beirut offered a chance to examine that proposition under fire. Would the children who spoke to me of conciliation when their lives were relatively peaceful hold the same view in the middle of a blitz? I wanted to find those children, and I was also eager to re-enter a circumstance in which life's importance is urgent and clarified.

Then too I had been bothered by a failure of mine ever since the story on the children was published. Several Lebanese-Americans, including representatives of the Lebanese embassy, had written to upbraid me for focusing exclusively on the Palestinian children in Lebanon, for not having spoken with the children of the Lebanese as well. One afternoon a man from the Lebanese embassy in Washington called my office to criticize me for this. He was gracious and polite. I was furious and loud, accusing him of trying to pervert a story about children into a political pamphlet. By the time of that call I had already begun to agree that I had indeed made a serious error of omission; thus my leaping, inexcusable rage. Beirut offered a chance to make amends.

Understanding these things, my wife Ginny encouraged me, against her fears and mine, to ask my editor, Ray Cave, if I could make the return. Ginny observed that I would never be satisfied with this story unless at least once I pursued it "into the fire." That is exactly how I felt. I phoned Ray on Sunday morning, June 20. He considered in dead silence for a full minute while I waited with the damp receiver pressed to my ear. Ray does nothing without deliberation, nor is he ever embarrassed by the absence of conversation; I had waited on his deep silences often before. When he gave his permission we both knew that as I prepared for the trip, each would have second thoughts, though neither expressed them at the time. Ginny also had second thoughts, especially after she and I informed the children of the decision at dinner Sunday night with all the fake gaiety at our disposal and recognized in the eyes of Carl and Amy the reflection of our own doubts. Even three-year-old John absorbed our apprehensiveness. After I returned, Ginny told me that he would stare at the bombing scenes on the evening news and then announce grandly for everyone, "My daddy is in Beirut."

On Wednesday, June 23, I was on my way back to Lebanon, accompanied, to my delight, by Bill Pierce. Characteristically, Pierce, who had not been assigned this trip, forced himself upon it. There might be danger, after all; how could he resist? Then too there were probably a few odds and ends that Bill did not yet know about Lebanon, this being his first visit. On he talked as we flew to London on the first leg of the journey. I had forgotten how he could talk. Fortunately, he was not seated next to me but to Dirck Halstead, the *Time* photographer who was sent to coordinate the photographic operations there. They could have chosen no better. Never have I seen an operator like Halstead. It was he who arranged our itinerary from New York to London to Cyprus to Beirut, he who got us aboard a container ship in Cyprus, he who paid off the captain so that we could travel "first-class," on a large area of deck space. He did all this and much more seemingly with a flick of one hand. On his other hand dwelt Ollie, a green dragon puppet who often handled the talking when Dirck was busy.

The morning before we headed for our container ship in Limassol, Pierce and I waited in the lobby of the Nicosia Hilton while Halstead checked the telex for news from Beirut. There was news. The previous day Jack Reynolds, a correspondent for NBC, reported seeing the driver of the car directly behind his own shot through the head by a sniper as they traveled from East to West Beirut. Reynolds had taken a back road. Bill Stewart, *Time*'s bureau chief in Beirut, advised us to go by the Museum Road. I did not know where the Museum Road was, but in the next few days that road would be familiar to me, as would other places named in the papers as danger spots or sites of destruction. For the moment, I tried to piece together the situation from the items on the telex. The Muzak in the hotel lobby played "I Got a Gal in Kalamazoo." Kalamazoo in Cyprus. Halstead kept coming and going with more information. Alexander Haig just resigned. Why? Philip Habib announced a "permanent cease-fire." Really? "I Got a Gal in Kalamazoo, zoo, zoo."

Last night the three of us dined in an outdoor fish restaurant in Nicosia. Pierce and Halstead swapped war stories in the warm evening, Halstead recollecting a time in Viet Nam when the Americans had accidentally dropped a bomb on a monastery and a convent. Halstead described the procession of monks and nuns slowly descending a hill after the bombs fell, holding parts of their bodies together and moaning in the dark. He could hear nothing but their moaning and the clicking of his Leica. We talked of the necessity of telling the plain truth in such situations, in both writing and pictures, of using the normal lens, not the close-up or wide-angle. I think each of us was more exhilarated than fearful at the prospect of Beirut. For myself I feared one thing primarily; I was afraid to look on the dead. Not once had I ever seen a dead person, not my father, not my grandparents; I had not seen them lying dead. I had seen the dying, which may be worse, and I was certain to see much dying in Beirut. Yet it was the image of the dead that frightened me. Perhaps this was the fear of looking upon finality, upon the stiff, cool end of everything, every ideal, hope, thought and promise.

Late in the afternoon of Saturday, June 26, we board the *Cierzo,* née *Laura,* in Limassol; one could make out the original name painted underneath the new one. All day we watched dazed passengers coming into Limassol from Lebanon, refugees from the bombings, walking together but not acknowledging each other. They were so weary. One boy was noticeable for his black T-shirt on which was misinscribed, "Make Love Not Ware." A treasure trove for literary analysts. We are told some of the voyages across took twenty-four hours. I pray ours will be faster. Joining us in our "first-class" section are Joe Reeves, a reporter from the Chicago *Tribune,* David Friend, a writer from *Life,* and a young fellow from UPI who looks both excited and anguished. Other passengers, returning to their homes, sit in clusters scattered along the steel decks, finding places on the ship that was not made for passengers. On the plane from New York to London, it did not feel as if we were headed for Lebanon, nor did it from London to Cyprus, but it does now, in the chug-rumble of the ship's engine and the low murmurs of the voyagers. To the east the Mediterranean stretches in one dark, still line.

Tomatoes and cucumbers. Halstead bought tomatoes and cucumbers ashore, along with oil and vinegar for the salad he intends to toss. White wine too, naturally. A salad bowl, of course. He plays a cassette of the film score of *Napoleon,* as Matthew Naythons played Schumann in Thailand. I begin to think all photographers live in a movie. No one talks, not even

Pierce. We face the back of the ship. A bunch of journalists, most of us strangers, feeling close to each other nonetheless, because we are heading for the same place to do the same thing. Before us the sun sets in a mute explosion, and the sky goes purple, the shore of Cyprus a string of white beads disappearing into the sky, and the sea into the sky as well; all one. I think I have never seen anything so lovely. The thought makes me anxious.

At night I take one of the available cabins, which is located beside the ship's engine room, a continuous thunderstorm of noise. I sleep fitfully in the tiny metal chamber barely wide enough for a cot, barely high enough to stand in. I doze and am awakened by a nightmare of my dead father; I am with him in the dream. At 3 A.M. I sit bolt upright and confront a pair of mad blue eyes staring at me in the blackness. I pull the cord for the light bulb. My observer is a circular pillow made in the shape of a huge cat's head, resting on a shelf. The ears are white, the pink face shagged with white strands of fabric. The cat is meant to look cheery. I sleep again and dream once more of my father. This time he announces he must go to Mexico with my sister. In his life my father never went to Mexico. And I have no sister.

At four-fifteen I am awake again, wondering if the mission I set for myself is achievable. How would I go about finding Lara, for instance? I saw her but once, and briefly, and did not speak with her in the funeral procession for her parents. All I have is a name. So too for Samer, whom I saw for a few minutes in Tyre with his father the PLO colonel, when the Israelis were not in charge of the town. What would happen to the family of a PLO commander-in-chief? The baby Palestine? Would anyone pay attention to the whereabouts of an infant in the middle of a war? And Ahmed. If he was alive, he would probably be defending a position somewhere. Would he be able to talk to me? Would he care to? I was not as important to his life as he was to mine. To every one of the children, in every country, I was only a passing moment. In my wildest dreams I

189

thought of rescuing the children from Beirut. But why should they wish to be rescued by me? The whole trip could be for nothing. The engines bang in and out of my thoughts. I sweat through my clothes.

At five-forty I am up for good. I rejoin Pierce and Joe Reeves lying wrapped in blankets like cocoons in the cold, predawn air. At seven the sun is up, the water a gleaming blue-black plane. I see the coast of Lebanon. Most passengers are awake now, sitting up where they slept, turned to the sunshine like heliotropic plants. At seven-fifty an Israeli gunboat stops our ship and two other ships at a short distance from ours. The gunboat glides from ship to ship like a cop in a bar, from suspect to suspect. I wonder how often this ceremony has been enacted here at sea: Egyptians, Greeks and Phoenicians searching each other's ships. Two hours later we drop anchor in Juniye, just north of Beirut, greeted by boys and girls diving off motorboats and a water-skier taking a jump. Someone has a radio; I think I hear the Chipmunks.

By noon we are in a taxi on the Museum Road, crawling from checkpoint to checkpoint in the midday heat, finally crossing the Green Line that separates the east and west halves of the city. Three hours and a three-hundred-dollar cab ride later, I am standing in front of the Commodore again, embracing Abu Said where I last saw him in September. Bill Stewart steps forward—a gracious, tidy man in his late forties, with a generous, good-scout face. He greets us with remarkable cheer; his apartment was bombed yesterday. Suddenly, we hear what sounds like another bombing, but it is only the booms of Israeli jets dropping a shower of pink leaflets warning all civilians to get out of West Beirut.

We devise a simple plan for tracking down the children. Abu Said volunteers to inquire through his sources about the fate of Colonel Azmi and Samer. In the afternoon I will ask Mahmoud Labadi, the PLO press spokesman who had been so helpful my first visit, if he could locate Ahmed, Lara and Palestine for me. As for the children I met in the Tel Zaatar Orphanage—Jamila,

190

Mona and Boutros—Abu Said surmises that they are still in the orphanage, which has not been hit by shelling. I intend to seek them out after I find the others, but it happens that I will not get to the orphanage. By the time I plan to do so, it will be the week's end, the Israelis will have cordoned off West Beirut and I will be locked outside the city.

The following morning, while waiting for word of the children, Pierce and I visit a hospital shelled in a raid of last Friday, the heaviest bombing of the war to that point. The hospital for mental and psychological diseases was hit directly on several sides in last Friday's raid, but except for dozens of tiny smashed windows, its main damage shows in a lateral gap high on a wall—the shape of a huge, expressionless mouth. When the twelve bombs landed on the drab, gray structure, six people were killed and twenty injured. Two female patients sitting in the lounge were sliced to pieces by the shrapnel. It could have been worse. A rocket that hit the children's ward got entangled in a blanket and miraculously never went off.

This is a private hospital for the aged as well as the mentally handicapped and retarded. Among its patients, the chief physician tells us, are Lebanese, Palestinians, Maronites, Druze, Sunnis, Shi'ites and Jews: "All Lebanon is here." An Armenian lies curled up on the second-floor landing. His stained white shirt hangs outside his blue pants. He wears a gray suit jacket, even in this heat. Flies collect on his bare feet. He pays no attention. He wants to sleep. "There was nothing," he explains when asked about the bombing. He is said to have gone wild when the shelling started.

In the children's quarter a wall cabinet displays a Fisher-Price xylophone, an inflated plastic goose, and a blond doll with her arms flung wide in surprise. The phosphorus bombs left long brown streaks on the ceiling. Two beds are charred like marshmallows. No children were in their beds when the bombs fell. Still, some tried to leap through the holes the shells created in the walls. They have been relocated near the women. Heads shaved, they seem of one sex or of none. Some are naked. They are penned in a small dark space; they smell of urine; their thighs are stained with excrement. Many moan continually. One boy shivers, another laughs. One cannot speak with these children. A woman lurches forward and shouts in English, "I am normal!" Another, somewhere, begins to keen like a siren warming up.

"This is the worst I have seen," says Hamil, seventy-five. He sits up in the bed in which he slept when the bombs fell.

"Were you in Lebanon during World War II?" I ask him.

"Yes, I was here. But in that war the world was not so crazy."

At the PLO office later that day, I ask Labadi if there is any progress on the children. He starts to answer when there is a swift, sudden commotion. Yasir Arafat enters the room seemingly from nowhere, surrounded by bodyguards. He appears diminished, weary; the energy seems forced. Labadi introduces me and invites me to ask questions. I doubt I will be up to this. As I begin, the reporters who have been waiting outside now crush through the office door and stand taking notes in a crowd.

"When the war stops, what happens to the Palestinians in Lebanon?"

"They remain to put their fingers on the main spokes of the Palestinian issue, the Palestinian cause, the Palestinian rights. We are human beings, and we have the right to live like human beings, with our dignity. We have the right of self-determination. We have the right to go back to our homeland. We have the right to establish our own state."

"Will you give up your arms to the Lebanese Army?"

"Would you give up *your* arms to the Lebanese Army?"

A rumor of the day has five Egyptian ships on the way to Beirut to help with the proposed evacuation of the Palestinians. Arafat is asked if he gets seasick. He laughs off the idea as "silly." As for leaving a limited force in Beirut, he says that remains to be discussed with the Lebanese. Would he, under any circumstances, enter into negotiations with Israel?

"Do you think we should negotiate with the Israeli, barbar-

192

ian, savage, terrorist military junta in Israel, with their hands full of blood?" His eyes strain forward. "Do you think? But I am here." He rises abruptly and goes to his car, flashing the V sign for the photographers outside.

Back at the hotel, I berate myself for not having served as a sharper interrogator. Arafat was the single principal war-maker I was to meet face to face on my journey. I ought to have slipped in at least one thoughtful, unpredictable question. Beside incompetence, I could blame only surprise. I had not imagined that so fiery and bellicose a public figure would, up close, look and sound like any sweating demagogue. I felt nothing for him, neither contempt nor satisfaction at his plight, which I was far more likely to feel. Israel was dead wrong to bomb Beirut, but the PLO had made that wrong possible. Men and women like Arafat create the children of war, are responsible for the condition I was probing. In their own distorted way they make the world go round. I wish there had been more to see.

At five-fifteen that afternoon Israeli jets roar high above the city. Two sonic booms follow in quick succession. A cloud of leaflets is produced in midair. It hangs, then floats down very slowly, like a great hive of small white birds beating their wings wildly as they fall.

The following day there is news of Lara. A few months after her parents were killed, the girl was taken to live with relatives in Jordan. She is said to be well. Nothing on four-year-old Samer or the baby Palestine yet, but Ahmed has been located. He is posted somewhere on the front. His older brother Farouk will try to track him down. Farouk is more self-assured than Ahmed, a bit colder as well. At thirty-one he holds a high rank in Al-Fatah, the largest faction within the PLO. He says very little to me at first, sizing up the stranger. Our taxi rolls past a fat man who has been forced to drop his pants for a search at a checkpoint in the middle of the street. He stands there helpless before a group of boy soldiers and squeals in rage and humiliation.

At Ahmed's home his parents are warm and hospitable.

Within minutes several of the family have gathered—sisters, brothers-in-law and their children—to talk with Pierce and me. Soldiers saunter in. The discussion starts out with guesses on Ahmed's whereabouts and soon swirls into everything from the Syrians to the weather to abstract politics. An old soldier suggests, "People are better than governments." Farouk gets an idea where Ahmed might be, and the taxi is off again, passing a mosque with a charred black wall on which some child has painted a bright blue plane dropping bright blue bombs. Rubbish burning everywhere heats the air from below as the relentless sun works from above. In a marketplace in a Palestinian camp, where Ahmed is at first thought to be located, a walleyed woman asks me furiously, "What do you think of these dogs, the Arabs?" A camp security guard points out a grape arbor on a roof and explains that Palestinians create such things "to express their relationship with their native home."

Ahmed is in Shuweifat, a Palestinian stronghold (a neighborhood, really) east of the Beirut airport. Both the Israelis and the Phalangists are encamped nearby, not five hundred yards away. It is close to noon. The streets are white, deserted. Overhead two jets, flying side by side, make a quotation mark as they veer. Ahmed enters the office to which he has been summoned. Thinner than in September, he is still boy-faced. He shakes hands with all the soldiers sitting around the room. He wears a camouflage suit, a pair of sneakers, and a cap that looks like a sun hat with the brim turned up, his PLO badge pinned to the front of it. He plunks down on a couch with a machine gun resting in his lap. Then he gives me the business for publishing the name of his girl friend Jomaneh in last winter's story. I tell him to watch his manners or the girl's address will be published this time.

"In September you said that you wanted to be a doctor. You also said that if you were at war with Israel and a wounded Israeli needed your help, you would behave as a doctor, not a soldier. Now that you are at war with Israel, do you say the same thing?"

"Yes." He is definite.

"What do you make of this war?"

"I cannot find the words. I don't hate the people. But I do hate the *actions* of the people."

He has turned sixteen and is all soldier now. He will not speculate on what course the PLO should take. "It is up to our leaders." Asked if it came to a choice between laying down his arms and living to fight another day, or fighting it out to the end, he says: "There is no alternative. If we lose our identity, we lose everything." When pressed for a choice between reason and honor, he says, after some thought: "If I have to make priorities, I would choose honor first, but I don't know the answer, really." Sitting beside his brother, Farouk chips in: "I would never place logic before dignity."

What would it take to secure peace in the area? I ask Farouk. "First," he says, "the Israelis would have to withdraw." A certain number of miles? "No. Completely."

"But they will not do that."

"Then war is inevitable. War is always inevitable when someone wants to take someone else's territory."

Would he lay down his arms if the PLO leadership ordered it? "They will not order that. And I will never give up my gun voluntarily. Not after all my sacrifices." There is no doubt he means it. His passion seems both national and personal. "The Israelis want everything. If I give them everything, I have nothing."

"Ahmed." I turn to him. "You are quite close to the Israelis here. Do you picture them in your mind?"

He smiles sadly. "I can actually see them." Asked if he imagines a sixteen-year-old like himself on the other side, he responds that he does not like to think of the Israelis as individuals. I hear a hardening in his tone, but I see none in his appearance. He seems to grow younger and frailer even as we talk. But we can talk no longer. He is called outside. As he rises he suddenly confronts me with the most perplexed expression. "Why did you travel all this way to talk with Ahmed?"

195

Because I love him, I tell him, which I realize, surprised at my answer, is true.

Out in the street, Ahmed points to the left, where the Phalangists are positioned, and to the Israelis on the right. Shuweifat is dead still; the apartment houses are still; the alleys like alleys in a painting. Suddenly there is a barrage of gunshots from the Phalangist side, but no one and nothing is hit. The PLO soldiers return the fire. A skinny cat runs for cover. A chicken rapidly crosses the road, answering at least one question. More gunfire, then silence. Ahmed must return to the others. He hesitates before saying good-bye, then goes off with his comrades, trotting back for a moment to place in my hand the badge from his cap. He apologizes that it is all he has to give.

Late that afternoon I learn that the baby Palestine is living safely with her father's sister's family in Syria. Oddly enough, however, a new Lebanese baby has just been born under similar circumstances. I see him in the hospital. The mother, shot in the abdomen, died as the child was delivered. The father is unknown. The boy, called Samer by the nurses, is olive-skinned and weighs barely four pounds. One has to hold him close to the chest to prevent him from slipping through.

The news of the next morning clatters through breakfast. The U.S. is trying to keep Israel from invading West Beirut; the Israeli Cabinet will hold a special session on Lebanon today; Israel will allow the PLO to leave Beirut carrying small weapons, but they *must* leave; Lebanese Christians and leftists go at each other in the mountains east of Beirut; Saudi Arabia's King Fahd telephones President Reagan. Will the day see more leaflets or the real McCoy? Reporters trade guesses around the Commodore swimming pool, where a trained parrot whistles the first four notes of Beethoven's Fifth. I begin to grow used to such things in Beirut. The swimming pool itself is a point of danger. Deep but empty, there is little room to walk around its sides. By the end of the week one man will have fallen in, severely injuring his head and breaking a leg, while another, in

196

a bizarre decision to jump to his rescue, will have broken his leg too.

Nearby, the Hotel Triomphe has been converted to an emergency hospital. Here, Abu Said tells me, I may find the Lebanese children I wished to speak with. In the unlit lobby restaurant twelve beds are set out where the tables once stood. A label on the door to the room indicates American Express cards are welcome. More patients lie upstairs. A Lebanese man named Said lay napping in his home when it was hit by a phosphorus bomb. His face glows pink where the layers of skin have been burned away. It seems wrapped in cellophane. Said's head is swathed in bandages, except for his ears, which protrude like pink knobs. He looks perpetually surprised, as if amazed at the removal of his face. He makes candies for a living. Beside him lies a Syrian in a crew cut who salutes me. He was out for a stroll when a shell hit the street. His right leg was blown off at the knee. He wonders if his fiancée will still love him.

I find no children in the Hotel Triomphe, but several Lebanese children have been brought to the Maqassad Hospital, a real hospital, where two hundred have died since the bombing began. Twelve-year-old Houda had her stomach slit open by shrapnel, but she feels well now and smiles to show it. She does not know what this war is about. I ask her how wars get started in the first place, and she explains that there are two kinds of people, the bad and the good. Then she considers for a moment: "Not all Israelis are bad." Then she corrects herself again. "All people are good." Her black eyes glow with confidence.

"Why do you think all this happened, Houda?"

"It is God's will," she says.

"Did God want the war to occur?"

"No. God never wants people to kill each other."

"Will God end the war, then?"

"If He wills."

The emergency nature of the cases has been hard on the hos-

197

pital staff. Only seven doctors are available for a hundred patients. Pierce and I sit with the doctors in a huddle as they describe, with no personal pride, the days without sleep. Five specialists had to work on one patient alone, so much of the man was either injured or missing. The patients who were transferred from the shelled mental hospital presented a particular problem. They would stare at their wounds and laugh aloud, or they would tear at their bandages. One man was brought in with part of his abdomen hanging outside his body. He was fully conscious. With his left hand he tried to scoop his intestines back inside.

A seventeen-year-old boy named Khalid had his testicles blown off. He used to work in a printing office. He and his father were hiding under their house when it was shelled. The doctor who treated Khalid introduces me to him. The boy smiles politely even as the doctor rolls down his sheets to display the raw, flat skin of his groin. "There is no purpose to war," says Khalid. "But no one is to blame, either. The Israelis were only taking orders." Asked if he seeks redress for his injury, he answers that he wants peace, not revenge.

"Why are you not angry?" I ask too earnestly. He looks at me with equal curiosity.

The doctor points out a thirteen-year-old girl named Waffa. She was asleep when her home fell on top of her. She is asleep now too. Her head is shaved where they operated. Her left ear is blackened, her left eye swollen red. Below it her cheek is sheathed in a purple-gray plaster. Her brain is damaged. She will be partly paralyzed for life. Beside her bed sits her older sister, who cannot bear to look. She stares instead at the open window. My daughter Amy, with her head shaved, would look a good deal like Waffa.

Noon at the Palestinian cemetery. The air is unusually cool under trees formed like umbrellas. Photographs of the dead are planted over the graves; they look like college yearbook pictures. Four new half-dug graves lie open in the red soil. The older ones are festooned with delicate paper petals and the

198

kinds of ribbons used on candy boxes. A discarded stretcher lies off in a corner beside a green hospital mask. There is shelling to the south. Back at the Commodore a message comes through that Colonel Azmi is reported killed in Tyre. Is the boy Samer alive?

On Thursday, July 1, Pierce, Halstead and I make an excursion across the Green Line into East Beirut. We are accompanied by David Rubinger, a *Time* photographer and an Israeli who has come north to join the *Time* staff covering the war. East Beirut has no war. Shops show pretty summer dresses. Beach balls hang in bright clusters in the toy stores. Hibiscus glows red in the dark green hedges. It is on high ground, East Beirut, the air almost cold. Except for the jeeps and the armored personnel carriers, we see nothing to remind us of the western half of the city.

At the bottom of a high hill the Beirut airport lies open and vacant except for the carcasses of two scorched jets on the runway. To the left stands Shuweifat, where I talked with Ahmed the day before yesterday and where he is on patrol now. Our vantage point is Israeli headquarters, a converted secondary school beside a music conservatory. Armored vehicles rest in the parking lot. It is here that I must arrange for an escort to the south, to Tyre, to try to find Samer. The trip is scheduled for Sunday. The Israeli officer is helpful. He laments the war. "The world has not been fair to the Palestinians." He tells of a Palestinian mother, the wife of a PLO officer, who escaped West Beirut with her baby and came to the Israeli headquarters for protection. Mother and child were cared for and escorted safely south to Nabatiye. The story is not told to create a good impression. The officer is fifty-eight, jaded, a former air force pilot. Having survived four crashes, he claims the right to optimism.

North to Byblos. Ads for Woody Allen movies and a curious recurring road sign, Baby Love Me, that seems to have no reference. Here one is yet farther from the war. Not a soldier in sight. Only the ancient city and the ancient port, still protected by a Crusader fortress. Kids in bathing suits dangle their legs from the tops of the walls. Pleasure boats bob in the water where the Phoenicians once sailed. At lunch at the Fishing Club restaurant, we chat with the owner, Pepe Abed, half-Mexican, half-Lebanese, who boasts pleasantly about the celebrities who have dined at his place, and produces a huge, elaborate guest book containing the autographs of Candice Bergen and David Niven. Before we depart, Abed insists that we inspect his museum-bar below the restaurant. We descend a flight of stairs into two cool, dark rooms displaying statuettes among the cocktail tables. Phoenician, Hittite, Greek, Roman, Persian; all snatched from the sea, the headless, armless relics of former powers. Of a Greek boy's face only the mouth and chin remain. We admire the frieze of a dying woman. I wonder which is Lebanon: West Beirut in the distance or this odd mixing of history and luxury?

Back in West Beirut by sundown, Pierce, Halstead and I tramp about the shelled sports stadium. The topmost stands have been crumbled like stale cake. The poles, where pennants flew, are bent and cracked. Great fissures mark the walls. The clock and scoreboard have been stopped cold. Gray stones are piled like giant's chalk where steps were, where millions once roared for the winners. We mount a boulder and gaze at the empty field. A dog trots back and forth in the shadows. More shots from somewhere. At 2 A.M. Israeli jets streak low over the hotel, creating astonishing booms. My ears ring, stunned. In the black sky two sulfurous flares glow sickly yellow, blaze momentarily, then disappear before an orange spray of machine gun bullets.

Pierce and I spend the two following days wandering in West Beirut, killing time before we head for Tyre and Sidon on Sunday. Friday morning I stop off at the PLO press office again, seeing it for the last time, though I do not know that then. Residents of the apartments above the office are hauling box springs and couches through the lobby. A man struggles to cram a crystal chandelier into the trunk of his Mercedes. Labadi has not yet arrived. Later I regretted not seeing him that day to say good-bye, but I never really worried about his safety, even during the ferocious bombings of July and August. Labadi is a practical man. I suspected (for no good reason) that he had nurtured a second identity somewhere, that one day I would bump into my pistol-packing propagandist emerging from a men's club on Fifth Avenue, sporting a Homburg and looking fresh as a scrubbed baby. How d'ye do, Mr. Labadi. It *is* Mr. Labadi?

Right now his office looks as if it had been deserted months ago, all the leaflets and printed slogans lying in paint powder on the shelves. Down the street, bombed so frequently, stores remain closed behind sheets of corrugated metal. Sandbags lie piled on oil drums. In the rubble of an apartment house I spot a pair of shoes in the Charlie Chaplin position. An officer finally arrives to announce that there will be a press conference on the subject of cluster bombs at 1 P.M. The PLO seeks to demonstrate that the Israelis are violating U.S. rules by using the American-made cluster bombs for offensive purposes. The casings are on display, as are the small steel pie wedges where the "bomblets" were contained. They are spread out on a table beside a small ornate chess set. The PLO knows that cluster bombs are an especially abhorrent weapon for the damage they do to innocents. We are told that each unexploded bomblet case contains a spring mechanism which enables the device to leap two feet in the air when touched, say, by a curious child. The bomblet thus goes off at just the right height. I try to picture what the bomb's designer looks like.

In the Sanayeh Gardens, the public gardens, refugees from bombed-out homes encamp under strange asparaguslike trees that bulge at the top. Families make walls with rugs and laundry strung with ropes. Not long ago this park was used almost exclusively by the city's rich. It reminds me of the Gramercy Park of my childhood: graceful pathways, bright flowers and wooden benches at the proper distance from one another. Here half-dressed babies waddle among their parents' last possessions. Shirts hang on bushes like oversize blossoms. A woman does her wash in a plastic bucket. Four elders play a game of cards in the shade. They are ashamed of their plight and shoo Pierce and me away.

Either there is great tragedy or great aimlessness. In another makeshift refugee camp, a modern secondary school, children drift in clusters from corner to corner in a large playground. Jomaneh, ten, explains that she had to leave her house "because all the windows were broken." No, she has no idea why people kill people. How to stop wars? "Live freely." The most beautiful thing in the world, Jomaneh says, would be to go home. Everybody waits: the PLO, the Israelis, the outside world. After a week of leaflets and flares, tension verges on boredom.

Why am I here, really? Why have I come all this way, and why am I now preparing to go to Tyre on an improbable quest? A four-year-old boy, his father dead. He does not know me. What can I tell him? What can he say to me that I have not heard over and over already, in every country on the first go-round and here again from Ahmed and the Lebanese children as well? There were no surprises from them. If I find Samer, there will be none from him either. Seeking out the boy offers a purpose in a purposeless place, but that hardly seems reason to have come to Lebanon. I told Ahmed I made the trip because I loved him. Did I therefore seek Samer because I loved him too, a boy at whom I looked for five minutes in both our lives?

When I considered this, I realized that all the reasons I had proposed and itemized for returning to Lebanon were secondary; valid and responsible but secondary. What I had come for was not to add new elements of information to a story, nor to satisfy myself that the children I knew were safe, nor to rescue them from harm, nor to determine if their peaceful disposition would be altered "in the fire." I had come to Lebanon to enter the fire myself, the core of the matter I had glimpsed in Athens. If I had learned what I wished to learn about the children while circling the world in the fall, still something remained to be seen at the center, where the fire is. Whatever it was drew me toward it like gravity, in the small person of Samer.

It then occurred to me that my quest was not personal. Rather, I felt like any adult in search of any child, of any child in trouble. Was I looking for the child in me as well? I was in trouble, all right. Every adult is in trouble in war. Adults did not come out very well in the stories the children told. But the world in the eyes of the child beholder is not in trouble, not yet. It is new and open to possibility. That, in part, is what this search was after: possibility and change. On the way over I recalled my lifelong fear of looking upon a dead person, but in fact I saw no dead person, not even here. Yet I looked upon the dead-as-ever world; unchanging, stiff as a board. Not so to Samer, however, not to the child. It was his view I wanted to find, and to retrieve.

Yet for what purpose? Even if it were possible to retrieve a child's way of looking at the world, the acquisition would be brief and temporary. A stock poetic dream is to wish oneself back to childhood, to try to get back whatever one was, or believed one was, before the fall. It presumes, of course, that there will be no fall the second time around. Were I in fact able, by a feat of alchemy, to exchange my view of the world for that of the children I met on my travels, for Khu's view, for instance, how long would it be before I felt the old hardening of the spirit again, my own rigor mortis? How long will it be before Khu himself begins to change? In September Samer told me he would love to live in a world without soldiers. Now history has brought him one year closer to being a soldier himself, whether he loves it or not.

At the beginning of this journey I thought about what I might learn. I wondered if talking with children of war would offer any sign of the future of their countries; whether the children would provide a sense of the meaning of war itself; whether they might even reveal why war exists. I now began to feel that these questions were futile. History made them futile. Two days ago I saw Ahmed, the boy who would value being a doctor over a soldier, functioning quite successfully as a soldier nonetheless. My hypothetical question was a game, a little melodrama. Of course, Ahmed would be a soldier in the crunch; his biography moved toward soldierhood from the moment he was born. However admirable his native instincts, generations of decisions had cast his life in bronze, just as Samer's life was cast, and mine, and Khu's too.

Until this point I think I had been drifting under the misapprehension that wars are volcanic eruptions in the otherwise placid motion of events. Now that I had glimpsed five wars in a sweep, all running concurrently, I was reminded that the institution was not a deflection of history, but history itself, that this is the way history is made. If anything, it is the placid periods, the doldrums, that disturb the flow of the universe. An ahistorical context. For the purposes of the story, I have been viewing children in an ahistorical context. Well, there is no ahistorical context. We *are* our wars. We gain national and social identities through wars. War is geography, biology, art. Why should I have presumed that the children of war, with all their goodness and mercy, might pervert these things when they grew up, when war gives them the initiation into adulthood itself?

Ahmed's brother, Farouk, surmised that wars occur when someone covets someone else's territory. But wars are brought on by a multitude of reasons, as I had chanced to observe in merely a few weeks in a single year in a single century noteworthy for hundreds of wars, perhaps a thousand wars, justified and unjustified, short and extended, pocket- and world-size. Even in the five little wars I witnessed, every motive for belligerence was on display, each going strong and also supported by an intricate and stable backup system; if one cause failed, another was ripe to take its place. Last September in this same country I deemed war a moral lie. I neglected to mention it is a lie we all share. Pure blindness combined with too great a concentration on the children had prevented me from concluding that war is the way the world progresses. Life wasn't Hong Kong; it was Lebanon. It was civil war and holy war and the war of aggression and the war of defense. How does violence grow in the heart? I asked at the outset. Irrelevant. Beside the point. A tidal wave accumulates water as it goes. It was mere fancy to think that any single element could turn the tide, much less explain its origins.

Still, one can't help but wonder where is the individual mind in this process. Once in a while, the world comes up with a singular hard-nose like Gandhi or Martin Luther King who does turn the tide. In the massive, inexorable scheme of war making, is one to conclude that these occasional tide turners are also part of the cosmic murder plot, that they are merely dropped on the earth to create brief rest periods before history finds its way again? One could easily believe such a thing in Lebanon, listening to the small, hospitalized voices proclaiming God's will and seeking peace with impotence, while all around them the destructiveness of the race locks them in a parenthesis. A little resistance is good for dramatic tension, after all; adds a moment of doubt before the house caves in. In every place I visited before returning to Lebanon, it was the children's voices that made the loudest noise. Not here. Things were in perspective here.

And yet even in Lebanon I heard quite clearly the voices of Khu, Hadara, Elizabeth and the others. Even in the place that showed history as it is, I heard them over the din. For in truth it was not them alone I was hearing. My own meek voice accompanied theirs. I realized here that whatever surprises the children of my journey offered me by their gentleness would not have been grasped so readily or so comfortably had I not some gentleness of my own, however camouflaged, with which to receive it. Nor was I unusual in this. Every adult responds to the gentleness of children. I noted this at the start, when I was preparing for the journey and was dutifully setting down all the reasons I could think of why children are important to adults. But I was wrong in a central assumption. I thought that children were important to grown-ups because grown-ups saw in them all they had lost in the process of becoming grown-ups. I knew now that children matter so much to adults because they remind us that we never lost the original gentleness at all, that we never lost any of the virtues of childhood. The acquisitions of size, power, zeal, authority and territory may have pushed our best feelings aside or below, but we did not really lose them. When I was astonished by Khu, I was astonished by what I recognized as still alive in myself. I was astonished by me.

The trick of living satisfactorily as an adult lies in being able to unearth that gentleness and to then apply it to a more complicated life. Such excavations take a lot of effort and desire, which may be why so few tide resisters crop up in the course of events. But could the effort be any greater than that of a twelve-year-old girl with her stomach slit open or of a seventeen-year-old boy with his manhood obliterated? It seemed to me that at least an equal effort was required to push one's gentleness away, to disguise its existence. It seemed that in retrospect, at any rate. For I looked at myself and saw it had been done quite well.

Yet the choice remained as long as life remained. Perhaps that is what I was seeking in Samer. Perhaps in looking at the boy I would be looking at the choice.

I begin Saturday, July 3, at 5 A.M., surveying the city from my hotel window and watching an old woman mop her balcony across the way. Finished, she stands and stares straight at me. The bulletin of the morning announces that the Israelis have closed the Green Line at the museum. It is necessary for Pierce and me to get to East Beirut right now, so as not to be locked in West Beirut tomorrow. I feel an odd wave of loss and regret at the prospect of leaving. For all its pain and destruction, West Beirut is where the world's heart beats at the moment, this parched, sunstruck, ruined place. Pierce and I say hasty goodbyes to our colleagues, for whom we fear. No one looks at anyone else directly or for long.

By four the following morning the car is ready to head south. It takes the long way around by the Damascus Road, passing an institute for the deaf along the way. The institute was shelled. What is it like not to be able to hear the shell that falls on you? In the backseat of the car sit two Israeli soldiers making muted conversation. Dan is our official escort. Eli goes along for the ride. He is a historian when not functioning as a chicken farmer on a kibbutz. He took his Ph.D. at the Sorbonne and teaches Jewish history part time at Tel Aviv University. No, he does not believe this is his nation's last war. "We are always among enemies." Eli is forty, but his full beard makes him look older. He is tall and heavy in the shoulders, a powerful soldier. A major now, he has fought for Israel in three wars. His son was close to tears when Eli went off to this one. Eli is not sure this war was necessary, but he will fight it. Among the people is, he most admires Anna, for his combination of faith and realism.

Later in the morning Dan will find Eli in despair. Eli will reach unconsciously into his breast pocket and pick out a playing card, the nine of hearts. Several days earlier he took it away from one of his men in order to prevent card playing on duty. The soldier from whom he took it was new to battle, quite young, and scared. He made an error of judgment the next day and was killed by a PLO sniper. Eli had forgotten about the card in his pocket.

As the car rolls south, Israeli trucks roll north. One has a feeling that a push is on. The car reaches Sidon by 8:30 A.M. So much is destroyed here. Yet there was always destruction in Sidon. It is hard to tell ancient ruins from modern ruins. The historian, Eli, does not mind seeing damaged stones: "Children, yes." Dan, an artist in civilian life, says that he could never paint any of this. His hair is entirely gray, but he looks younger than Eli. He rarely speaks. In the dust beside a crushed house an Israeli captain discovers a one-mil coin marked "Palestine" and dated 1942. When it was used as currency, the whole world was at war. I wonder who preserved the coin in Sidon.

Above the city, on a high hill, stands a ten-story statue of the Virgin holding the baby Jesus. A metal halo is riveted over the

Virgin's head. One can enter the monument at the base and climb up inside it, inside the mother and child. Dan and I do so, hesitating at the top because the protective wall has been shot away. This was a recent PLO position. An antiaircraft gun was mounted here. Below the Virgin, the Israeli soldiers mill. "I hate war," says Dan out of the blue.

In Tyre at last I make initial inquiries at Israeli headquarters whether anyone knows where Colonel Azmi's family might be. The commander suggests that the Greek bishop would have some information; it is believed that Azmi's wife and Samer lived with the bishop for a time after the colonel was reported killed. The bishop says no; he thinks that Mrs. Azmi stayed with a Roman Catholic priest for a while. It is so. The priest says that she and Samer lived with him two weeks, but that they left two days ago to stay with friends. He provides an address.

The apartment house is in a shady alley. Two women come to the door and appear friendly but apprehensive. Yes, Samer and Mrs. Azmi were there in the building, but they are gone now. They have moved to a town outside the city, which the women name. I return to the others and learn there is no such town on the map.

An Israeli officer suggests the probable: "You will never find the boy. First, no one is absolutely sure that Azmi is dead. The burned body they discovered was only assumed to be his. So the woman will be waiting for him, and she will want to stay clear of strangers. Second, her husband was a well-known leader. She probably fears for her life. You would be looking for the kid forever." I know he is right. Still, I feel compelled to poke around Tyre a little while longer, peering foolishly into the faces of four-year-olds.

There is one last place I wish to see: the roof of the bunker where Samer and Colonel Azmi were encountered last September. At the time, this roof was a room, an office, with straw walls, a straw roof, furniture and people. Over there stood the colonel's Swedish-modern desk, disproportionately large and stylish. And there the red fake-leather chairs were positioned

with their backs to the walls on two sides of the office. And
there sat the colonel's men, nodding approvingly at his harangue. He was a first-class haranguer, the colonel. He had the
eyes for it and the fists. He could thrust his body forward like
a cannon or draw back his chest in open innocence, a gesture
embellished with a "Why me?" look. Even now the pop of his
words reverberates in the memory.

But only in the memory. The colonel is not here. The desk is
not here. Nor the men, nor the roof, nor the walls. Nothing
remains on top of this bunker anymore, including a portion of
the roof itself, heaved high in a corner by an Israeli artillery hit.
Where the colonel delivered his harangue, the noon sun drills.
There is nothing else but silence and loose straw. No one who
did not know what function the straw originally served could
possibly guess that this was once a place of importance.

Pierce watches me patrol the room. I am too self-absorbed to
talk to him, but Pierce takes no offense. We understand each
other now. He is tolerant of my bad manners, and I have deep
affection for him. But I am lost at the moment, hearing only a
conversation that occurred a long time ago.

"Who is Sadat?" the colonel asked the boy.

"Sadat sold Palestine to Israel."

"Who is Jimmy Carter?"

"Carter supported Israel."

"Who are *you?*" The colonel regarded Samer with feigned
intensity.

"I am from Palestine," fired back his son. "From Hebron!"

It was then that Samer said he would love to live in a world
without soldiers. He said so there, standing where the Swedish-
modern desk was, where the straw shifts back and forth now.
After the boy left the room his father swore, "If I am killed,
my son will carry my gun."

With the walls down I can clearly see the Mediterranean
from the roof, not five hundred yards to the west. I sail the blue
water in my mind; first into the past, then north up the coast to
where the past is now, to the besieged city with its sonic booms

and rubbish fires and damaged children. Two of those I sought are known to be safely out of Lebanon. One is well in Beirut, though in a perilous position. The fourth is probably all right, in hiding with his mother, who will be protected by her people for being the widow of a warrior and hero. Nothing remains for me to discover or to do except to return to my own life.

My mind continues to sail in the white heat. Silently, in slow motion, the colonel's office rises back to its original shape. But the colonel is away today, and his men are not here either. It is Samer sitting behind the Swedish-modern desk, his head barely showing over the top. This time it is I who enter the room to stand at attention. The boy looks me over with deep curiosity. "Who are *you?*" he asks, as if he were his father. He is puzzled by the absence of an answer.

By three-thirty that afternoon I am in Israel again, speeding by taxi through that same part of the country where I talked with Hadara, Dror and Nimrod nine months earlier. By eleven I stand, bags in hand, at Ben Gurion Airport, ready to board the plane that would take me home for good. The date is July 4th. So ends my journey. Several weeks later I heard from Bill Stewart that Samer and his mother had fled to Damascus and were living there with friends. Several weeks after that the PLO pulled out of West Beirut, firing their guns in the air as they departed. I caught glimpses of Labadi on television, always beside Arafat, translating and advising. Once I saw Farouk on television very briefly in a pack of soldiers. Two months ago, in October, I heard from Ahmed himself. He is in Sofia, Bulgaria, studying medicine. In his letter he apologizes for his "so-and-so English," and wishes me "good time" in everything I do.

In the months since I returned from my two trips, little has changed in the countries I visited, with the notable exception of Lebanon. Even Lebanon cannot be said to have changed that much, since the interior battles now waged between Christians and Moslems are but revivals of the civil wars of the mid-1970s. No fighting goes on between Israel and the PLO these

210

days, but it is a question as to whether by expelling the PLO from Lebanon and devastating West Beirut, Israel has in fact secured its position in the Middle East. Viet Nam has started launching attacks against Cambodians encamped in Thailand, while in Cambodia itself a four-way war has replaced a two-way war and the people remain trapped in an expanded middle. In Northern Ireland, bombs go off regularly as ever. Some are transported to London, where earlier this year they blew off the limbs of palace guards and bequeathed an array of dead horses.

All this continues in the name of causes. The people go, but the causes survive. The children also survive. Quiet citizens, they go about their business, living partly in the world of affairs but mainly outside. In Belfast, Paul rides his five-speed racer, Keith studies diligently, Elizabeth skates at the disco. In Israel, Nimrod worries about the plight of the American Indian, while Dror concentrates on math and Nabil on tennis. The baby Palestine may be walking upright now, and Ahmed may dream of the lovely Jomaneh. At Khao I Dang, Nep Phem paints and Meng Mom dances. In western Massachusetts, Ty Kim Seng will pack his first snowball this year.

These are the children of war, but they are also ordinary children—a four- and five-foot civilization bearing books and lunch pails, dressed in school uniforms and preposterous T-shirts, sitting in the backs of cars, camping at windows and watching. Outsized by adults, they are not yet a constituency; they pose no threat. Will Joseph join the terrorists? Will Boutros? For that matter, will Heather and Hadara continue to crave peace? No one knows, least of all the children themselves, who have seen enough of change to respect it. Disappointing as it would have been to his father the colonel, Samer may leave the gun where it lies.

For the moment, these children are in the hands of others. They are the moved-from-place-to-place, the coaxed and hidden, the dragged-along and swung-into-the-sky, the hugged, the tickled, the slapped, the taught, the scolded, teased, praised, and sometimes the shot-at, and sometimes the decapitated and the killed-for-food. All that can be done to them is done, and they do what they are told. But not forever. One morning the streets through which they skitter now will be theirs to command. They will not think what to do; they will already know. Whatever becomes of them and of their countries will have been decided in some absolutely innocuous moment during these innocuous years, a moment they will not be able to trace. Their thinking done, they will rule largely by reflex, just as their parents did before them. Even Khu. Even Khu will rule by reflex.

Not that he considers such things now, of course, waiting in Hong Kong where I left him. Khu has never heard of the IRA or PLO or Israel or Lebanon. The name Ireland has no meaning to him, nor Poland, nor Nicaragua, nor any other distant place except America, which is closed to him, and which has no particularly clear image for him either other than that country where it is said one may be happy. His immediate wishes are sufficient: to get a bit more sleep, and to rid himself of the nightmare that the boat master will break out of jail and once again go for his head. Whatever else he thinks, he does not say, sitting by himself in front of the television set, or pacing the walkway beside the fence, or facing the harbor full of boats that sail the world where everything is beautiful.

Y

WITHDRAWN